CHRISTIAN EDUCATION IN MISSION

STUDIES ON THE CHURCH FOR OTHERS

STUDIES ON THE CHURCH FOR OTHERS is a series that explores the way in which Bonhoeffer's phrase "man for others" can be used as a description of the other-directedness of the church as it participates in God's mission in the world. Its purpose is to apply the perspectives and structures of the church-in-mission, which have grown out of the World Council of Churches' Study on the Missionary Structures of the Congregation, to specific areas of church life such as Christian education, worship, ministry. In this way the series seeks to make a contribution to the ongoing dialogue concerning the development of new forms of practical theology that fit the new shapes of the church as it serves the world today.

HANS HOEKENDIJK

LETTY M. RUSSELL, *Editors*

CHRISTIAN EDUCATION IN MISSION

by
Letty M. Russell

THE WESTMINSTER PRESS
Philadelphia

LIBRARY OF CONGRESS CATALOG CARD NO. 67–10926

Published by The Westminster Press ®
Philadelphia, Pennsylvania

PRINTED IN THE UNITED STATES OF AMERICA

To the Members and Friends
of
The East Harlem Protestant Parish
and
The Missionary Structure Study

CONTENTS

8 CONTENTS

INTRODUCTION

1. Giving thanks for the abundance of God's grace

"Rejoice always, pray constantly, give thanks in all circumstances; for this is the will of God in Christ Jesus for you." (I Thess. 5:16–18.)

In spite of "wars and rumors of wars"; in spite of "tribulation and distress"; in spite of those who with long faces "bind heavy burdens, hard to bear, and lay them on men's shoulders," the theme of this book is giving "thanks in all circumstances." For this is the purpose of the Christian life—the celebration of the fact that God in Jesus Christ has led men from bondage to freedom. And this is the purpose of Christian education—that men might live with joy and thanksgiving for what God has done and is doing in their lives.

Some of the readers of this book may wonder about its lack of emphasis on the rough edges of life. They may ask: Where is the tension between evil and good? between church and world? between failure and forgiveness? The answer to such questions lies in two directions: that of my experience and that of my theology. My experience is that of life in a Christian community set in the midst of poverty, failure, and despair that has nevertheless learned to give thanks (Eph. 5:15–20). My theology is based on the conviction that the resurrection and victory of Christ is the starting and ending point of Christian life and nurture (I Cor. 15:51–58). Certainly this does not mean that I am unaware of the insurmountable problems of the world in which we live, or of the fact that it is only by faith that we can declare that the world has been redeemed in Jesus Christ. Yet with Paul, I am convinced that "in everything God works for good with those who love him," not because sin and death do not abound, but because by the power of God "the grace of that one man Jesus Christ abounded for many" (Rom. 8:28; 5:15–17).

2. Experience in the East Harlem Protestant Parish

This book is written in the light of fourteen years' experience as teacher and pastor in the East Harlem Protestant Parish. Although it is *not* a description of life in East Harlem, or even of Christian education in the inner city, it is a product of theological reflection in this context. Such reflection has led me to two perspectives that are evident in this book. One is that by God's grace *men of faith can look at the world through "rose-colored glasses."* Because of God's grace, men can seek amidst evil and chaos to see what it is that God has called them to do, and how it is that God might be bringing about cause for thanksgiving even in a moment of despair.

This was first brought home to me when I reacted violently to those who viewed the problems of the inner city as an endless source of despair and hopelessness, leading to the defeat and retreat of many Protestant churches to the more agreeable middle-class culture of the suburbs.[1] It seemed to me that the city was a gift, and it was only by viewing it as a gift that men could come to love it, to understand its problems, and to seek to make it a place where men could find true humanity. When you begin to look at things in terms of how God's grace might be operative in and through them, you soon find: that Christian education is not just a stumbling block, but an opportunity to participate in Christ's invitation to join in God's mission; that peer-group behavior of youth and adults in American culture is not just a denial of individual freedom, but an opportunity to work in terms of meaningful community life; that out-of-date structures of church life are not just a sign of the death of the church, but an opportunity to seek new structures more relevant to the modern world and more faithful to God's calling to witness to his love for that world. In short, you find with Paul that you can "give thanks in all circumstances; for this is the will of God in Christ Jesus for you" (I Thess. 5:18).

These "rose-colored glasses" are known as *eyes of faith*. Paul Minear calls eyes of faith the "angle of vision," "focus of vision," and the "horizon of vision of the Bible."[2] They are the way that a Christian looks at the world in terms of his faith. He sees God at work in and through the events of this world because God's revelation of Jesus Christ has helped him to see these events as part of his plan and purpose for the world (Luke 24:28–35). God explains to Isaiah (ch. 6) that the eyes of faith are exactly what the people of Israel do not have: "Go, and say to this people: 'Hear and hear, but do not understand; see and see, but do not perceive . . . and turn and be healed.' " (Isa. 6:9.) The eyes of faith see both judgment and forgiveness. They see the world as it is, as God's world where men are redeemed, yet refuse to accept this gift of love. To see by faith and to live by faith is not to claim that other men see this way, but merely to say that this is the way that the Christian community reads history in the light of Jesus Christ.

Eyes of faith look at the world from the point of view of *salvation history*. They see the way God was and is at work in history, saving men from bondage and for freedom to live in a relationship of love and obedience to God and love and service to neighbor. Salvation history is the "horizon of vision of the Bible." It is not the only perspective of the Bible or the only way to understand its message. Other perspectives are possible as a way of interpreting the events of salvation. Yet it is a central theme that links both the Old and the New Testament as they assert that God is at work in history and that his concrete actions in and through Israel, Jesus Christ, and the church have significance for all of world history.[3]

Two other cautions that concern the use of the concept of salvation history should also be mentioned. One is the danger of equating salvation history and church history. The church has no history of its own. Its own life only serves as an "eyes of faith" perspective on the events of the world in which it witnesses to God's activity in and for the world. The other danger is that of equating salvation history with history as such and making it simply equal to process or change. Salvation history is not just history. It is the record of the way God is at work in and through history as he uses the events of history as part of his plan and purpose. Therefore it is not possible to point to particular processes in history, such as urbanization, racial revolution, secularization, and speak of them as salvation history or as the partial realization of the Kingdom of God. It is only possible to say that through the "horizon of vision of the Bible" we can see God at work in these events. Such a view of history is not the only perspective, but it is one that makes sense of my experience as part of a witnessing community which seeks to participate in the dialogue between God and his world with eyes and ears of faith.

The other perspective of this book, which is a result of theological reflection in the context of a witnessing community in East Harlem, is that the life of a witnessing community is a unity. Like Christian theology, *Christian ecclesiology is a unity in which the various parts are simply different perspectives on the same whole.* Our understanding of Christian community begins and ends with Christ, for it is in Christ that God has revealed his love for the world and called men and women to proclaim this love to all men. Thus when we speak of Christian faith, Christian worship, Christian education, Christian ethics, Christian witness, we are speaking of the same whole. In each case we are expressing a different perspective on the way men respond to God's grace with thanksgiving. They acknowledge God's grace, celebrate his grace, grow in his grace, live by his grace, share the fruits of his grace with all men. My discussion of Christian education begins with this assumption that in fact education is involved in the whole of church life, and ceases to be education when it is taken out of the context of the witnessing community.

Everything that happens in the witnessing community, be it faithful or unfaithful, is part of the educational process of Christian nurture of its members. This does not mean that education is more important or more inclusive than mission, worship, ethics, etc., but simply that it is important to recognize that everything that happens has an effect on the educational life of the community, in the same way that it affects community life in terms of witness, worship, service, etc. In this book no claim is made for education as the totality of all the parts of church life. But it is assumed that everything that happens in a Christian community should be viewed in an educational perspective if we are to understand how it is that Christ nurtures his people through their life together.

3. Experience in the study of Missionary Structures of the Congregation

This book is written not only in the light of my experience as a teacher and pastor in the East Harlem Protestant Parish, but also in the light of five years' experience as a member of the Working Committee on Studies in Evangelism of the World Council of Churches. This committee is engaged in conducting a worldwide study concerning "The Missionary Structures of the Congregation."[4]

Although this book is not a report of the content of that study, it is a product of theological reflection in that context. Such reflection has led me to three perspectives that are seen in this book. These perspectives are not unique to me because they represent not only the chronology of my thinking in the matter but also the chronology of the World Council of Churches' reflection on the meaning of evangelism in the light of the structures of the congregation.

The first perspective is that of mission as *God's mission*. The mission of the church is to participate in God's mission of reconciling the world to himself through Jesus Christ. It is God's mission that is the perspective for the church's self-understanding, for the church is called to be a witnessing community, joining in God's work of restoring men to their true humanity. The second perspective is that of *the world of history as the arena of God's mission*. God is at work in his world. His Word is addressed to the world. The church finds its place simply as a postscript to God's action in the world. Its job is to point to what God is doing by its own actions and life. Because the world is the arena of God's action, the church is called to take the world seriously and to ask itself in what way it can speak meaningfully and relevantly of what God is doing in its words and actions. The third perspective is that of the need for *new structures in the life of the church*. The present organization of local congregations and the present denominational structures are not adequate to the task of joining in God's mission or of taking the world seriously. Theological ideas, be they old or new, are not able in themselves to change the life of the church. Change must come as ideas are made reality in the social structures in which men witness and serve. The form of Christian community must take new shapes according to our understanding of God's plan and purpose for his world, and our understanding of the necessary social structures needed to do the job in a modern society.

The task of reshaping the life and message of the church seems almost impossible, as the "death of God" and "death of church" theologians are quick to point out. Yet this book affirms that "in everything God works for good with those who love him." In the face of the impossible, we must turn with eyes of faith to Him who makes all things possible and seek again the way to faithful witness and service.

PART ONE

Christian Education—
A Gift of God's Love

Matthew 7:9–11

"Or what man of you, if his son asks him for bread, will give him a stone? Or if he asks for a fish, will give him a serpent? If you then, who are evil, know how to give good gifts to your children, how much more will your Father who is in heaven give good things to those who ask him!"

This short simile on the "good gifts" of the Father appears in both Matthew and Luke as a saying concerning the fact that God answers prayer. However, it seems more likely that the original saying was addressed to the Pharisees, not to the disciples, and that it concerned Jesus' justification of his gospel for the poor and despised[1] (Matt. 12:11, 34; Luke 11:9–20). Jesus points out that even the Pharisees know how to give good gifts to their children. They do not give their children a stone instead of a loaf of bread, or a serpent instead of a fish. Why then should they be surprised that, with Jesus' coming, God bestows on his children (all who ask) the good gifts of the New Age (Matt. 11:1–6)?

We live in this new age—the age of Christ's coming when the gifts of God are offered to us. His greatest gift is that of his love by which he forms us and nurtures us and makes us his children (Gal. 4:3–7). Yet all too often the church, like the Pharisees, seeks to restrict this gift and use it for its own self-interest. In so doing, the church denies that the Father has given *good* gifts, and turns the "bread of life" into a stone.

Christian education is concerned with God's good gifts, for it is one of the ways in which people can participate in the gift of God's love. When it appears to be more like a "stone" than "bread" in the nurture of the Christian life, it is time for the church to search out ways that will allow God's children of the twentieth century to participate once again in the gift of love and nurture offered them by God.

1

CHRISTIAN EDUCATION AS BREAD
INSTEAD OF STONE

1. Christian education viewed as a possession of the church

SOMETHING IS WRONG with Christian education. It is not just that it is *too* practical, with not enough theology or Biblical exegesis. It is not that it is *not* practical with not enough psychology and educational expertise. In spite of its many reformations since its formal beginnings in the nineteenth century, Christian education today is so much like a "stone" in the minds of many church leaders that they have chosen simply to ignore it.[1] Such a statement needs little documentation. All that is necessary is to declare openly that you are studying or writing about Christian education, or to invite someone to a meeting about Christian education, and face the bored silence that follows. For Christian education in both theory and practice today seems to be like a great weight around the necks of those who think the gospel should be a thing of joy and freedom in which men respond fully in giving their lives in service to Christ and their brothers.

Christian education has always been a concern of the church, for it is the way by which men and women are nurtured in the Christian life. It is only since the comparatively recent development of the Sunday school that it has become a separate discipline. And this more recent development has been unfortunate, for it has focused attention in terms of nurture on one small aspect of life and reduced it to a tool for educating children and youth. For this reason, Christian education as a separate discipline never seems to have been exactly on the right foot. After earlier beginnings, in 1780 Robert Raikes organized Sunday schools as a systematic attempt to reach poor and unschooled with education in reading, writing, and arithmetic and in Christian fundamentals. Yet this Sunday school movement was only a small "Band-Aid" on the problems of the time—the problem of the children who had to go to school on Sunday because they worked in factories all week long; the problems and unmet needs of the new working classes who crowded the cities with the beginning of the industrial revolution.

Then Christian nurture became an alternative to revivalism in the churches of the late nineteenth century as Horace Bushnell advocated an understanding of the church as an extension of the Christian family where children could grow up as Christians. Again its importance was seen as a "Band-Aid" for church extension—an alternative evangelistic device for the recruitment of church members through sound Christian education that could be used by those who would not or could not depend on revivalistic preaching to bring the sheep into the fold.[2] Gradually in the early twentieth century in America, the emphasis shifted in Christian education to the stress on the Sunday school as an agent of moral education which in cooperation with the public schools would train citizens for American democracy.[3] It became a moral "Band-Aid" for American society. And all attempts at reform since then toward more emphasis on orthodox theology, the use of the Bible, and toward cooperation with the family, have not served to dislodge from the minds of the American public or from the American churches the idea that Christian education is to help make good people.[4]

Thus it becomes clear that one of the things that is wrong with Christian education is that it has become a captive of the church. It appears as a possession of the church that is applied as a "Band-Aid" to various problems of institutional survival. The church thought that maybe Sunday schools would somehow help them make church members of the new proletariat. Or it thought that it was a way of converting the next generation of church members who did not respond to other evangelistic methods. Or it thought it was a way to help make America a "Christian democracy." Time and again the church put down on paper its theological premise that only God makes Christians and then proceeded to design methods of Christian education that seemed to rule out that the education involved the gift of God's love. In spite of many very creative efforts at reform, Christian education has remained for the most part, not a way of participating in the gift of God's love offered to all his children, but as a possession of the church. This possession is largely offered to those lucky children whose parents think that the effort to get them to church on Sunday morning is justified by good training in middle-class morals which they receive. Thus frequently a "stone" is offered to God's children instead of the bread of life (Matt. 7:9–11).

A second thing that is wrong with Christian education is that separating it from other parts of church life has denied the unity of the church. Of course, everyone knows that the various aspects of church life *belong* together. But, for the sake of educational efficiency, we talk about educating children, youth, adults, seminary students as though they were completely separate and distinct, and we end up by contributing to the segregation of life and society into artificial age groups. For the sake of administrative efficiency we divide the mission of the church into evangelism, home missions, foreign missions, church extension, Christian education, pastoral care, etc., and suddenly end up thinking about God's love as coming all wrapped up in little packages to be offered to the people in the appropriate categories. Thus Christian education is compartmentalized so that it is seen as a piecemeal gift offered piecemeal to a man trying desperately to be whole. The church's need to make things fit into its scheme for institutional survival and efficiency has ended up in turning one of the gifts of God's love not only into a stone but into a series of small pebbles that it casts at random into men's lives.

One of the ways in which Christian educators have tried to make education more effective in the local church is by isolating it as a very specific intellectual discipline, so that the tools of education can be carefully designed for the task of teaching.[5] For instance, John Fry in his book *A Hard Look at Adult Christian Education* says that the educational job of the church is not evangelism or pastoral care, but to be a "small university" that teaches thinking men to think.[6] Certainly it is important to concentrate on particular intellectual tools that can combat the inadequate teaching methods that usually pass for Christian education programs in the churches. Such a development is parallel to the attempt of secular education to stop making claims for character development and educating the whole child and concentrate on tools of learning.

Even in secular education, however, this development flies in the face of the fact that neither children nor adults are just "minds" and that their total environment and culture has a powerful influence on their ability to learn. For instance, it is the subculture of poverty and segregation that is at the root of ghetto children's inability to learn and not their mental capacity.[7] It is equally as important that teaching tools used in the schools take into account the cultural attitudes of both the pupils and the teachers as that they take into account the fastest way to learn arithmetic. In the area of Christian education, tools are important, but they are not the most important factor. The most important factor is the way men, women, and children are enabled to participate in the gift of God's love. The context of this participation is the witnessing community, and the structure or organization of this community has great educational significance. Where the community itself fails to participate in the gift of God's love, teaching may occur, but the power and possibility of living by God's grace is less likely to be experienced, and the child or adult may never know that God has offered him the opportunity and power of joining in God's mission of reconciliation in the world. A church can become a stumbling block when it views itself as the possessor of the gift of education. In searching for the best tools for participating in the teaching process, it should not forget that education is a part of the gift of God's love.

2. Christian education as one of God's gifts

Christian education is not a gift that *belongs* to the church. It is a gift of God's love to all his children in which the church participates. It is a way in which God in Jesus Christ forms us by his love and makes us his children (Luke 11:13; Gal. 4:3–7). In this work it is Christ who is the teacher, working through his Spirit to bring us to full humanity as God's sons (Rom. 8:15–17; Eph. 1:5). It is Christ's discipline and instruction that makes us disciples who let our lives be shaped by his love (Eph. 6:4; Matt. 11:29). Christ is not only *the teacher* but he is also *the content* of the teaching (Eph. 4:20–21).[8] The events of his life reveal God's plan of salvation and form the gospel message that God has loved us and accepted us as his children. The Christian congregation does not own God's gift and it is not the educator. It is a participant in the gift of God's love and as such becomes simply the *context,* the "family of God" where God nurtures his children in Christ (Eph. 2:19–20). And its educational role is not to be the teacher but to join as a partner with all who are being educated, working together with them. Thus Paul defines his work with the Corinthians, not in terms of lording over their faith, but as working with them for their joy (II Cor. 1:24).

John Fry is pessimistic about any educational program

that assumes that men want to learn and that they can respond to the call to be educated.[9] Such pessimism might spring from men's inability to learn in isolation from the experience of God's love in a witnessing community.[10] Yet it is possible to be optimistic, not about what men can accomplish, but about the power of Christ as the teacher in a Christian community where his love is experienced as it calls men to participate in sharing that love through witness and service. When Christian education is viewed as a gift of God's grace, there is reason for "optimism" because we may be confident that God offers "good gifts" and not "a stone."

3. Christian education as participation in Christ's invitation

If Christian education is a participation in the gift of God's love, it follows that it is related to all the other parts of church life which also participate in that love (Luke 11:13). As a topic of study and discussion it can be separated from other parts of the life and work of the church, but it cannot be separated in fact or in action from the total work of Christ. In my own experience as a director of Christian education, I was led, after two years of trying to keep Christian education from being one compartment of church life, to seek ordination. I wanted to be a minister so that I would have the right to say that education was part of everything that happened in a Christian congregation where Christ was equipping his people for their service in the world (Eph. 4:11–12).

Christian education ceases to be Christian education as soon as it is compartmentalized, for it is part of the total gift of God's love working in the life of the Christian community by the power of Jesus Christ. The gift of love is Christ's invitation to all men to experience the power of God's gracious love which can restore them to their true human relationship of love and obedience to God, and love and service to their fellow men. It is Christ's invitation to all men to experience this power as they join in God's mission and plan for his world of restoring all men to their true humanity. Participation in this invitation of Christ is the basis of Christian education that can be defined as a way we can participate in the gift of love or, more fully, as a *way we can participate in Christ's invitation to all men, women, and children to join in God's mission of restoring men to their true humanity by reconciling them to himself and one another.*

Charles H. Dodd in his book *The Apostolic Preaching* has drawn sharp distinctions between *kerygma* (preaching the gospel to the non-Christian world) and *didache* (ethical instruction in the disciplines of the Christian life).[11] But it is clearly evident in the New Testament that the preaching of the gospel was immediately associated with a pattern of instruction in "walking worthy" of the Lord (I Thess. 2:11–12).[12] In fact the two words, *kerygma* and *didache,* are used in close parallelism with each other (Matt. 4:23; 9:35; 11:1; Acts 28:31). This is because there is no distinction in the gift of God's love that shapes men as disciples of Christ. To proclaim the gospel is also to teach what the gospel means. To teach about Christ is to proclaim the good news. Education in a Christian perspective cannot be placed in a separate category just because it is part of the gospel itself—it is the way that Christ invites men to join in God's work of reconciliation (II Cor. 5:10 ff.). As all the members of the church participate in this invitation of Christ, they become partners in extending the invitation and in hearing it and in responding. There is no longer any separation between the teachers and pupils, between preachers and teachers, between Christians and non-Christians, between study and action, for all are one in Christ's invitation—an invitation to freedom in joining God's work of reconciling men to their true humanity—an invitation to participate in the gift of God's love.

CHRISTIAN EDUCATION IN THE CONTEXT OF A WORLD OF CHANGE

1. A world of process and change

THE WORLD in which we live is no longer a world of place. The fact that it is made up of a series of small geographical units becomes less and less significant as modern technology binds it into one in terms of political, economic, and scientific developments. The most important thing about this world is not its geography, but its history. This is because it is a world of crisis and change—a world where events shape men's lives; a world where men, nations, God (and even the church) are in constant movement. Some philosophers have long since found this out. They have said that if things are makable, the course of events must be changeable. Men can make events even as they are part of those events.[1] But the Christian church, in continuing to live in a world of absolutes, has placed itself outside the world of history and has spent much more time and energy in trying to "stop the clock" or "ignore the clock" instead of finding out what it means to be "part of the clock."

We live in a world that is exploding in a technological revolution—a world which Arend van Leeuwen, in his book *Christianity in World History,* calls a technocratic world. There he points out that technocracy is a child of Western civilization.[2] One root is to be found in the theocratic understanding of the Hebrew God of the exodus who is not part of a cosmic totality (ontocracy) embodying nature and society. The Hebrew God is one who moves and is independent of the world—a God who makes events of history happen.[3] Another root is to be found in the Greek understanding of the world through Logos (rational mastery of the mysteries), which recognizes that man is capable of rational thought independent of the tyranny of gods and traditions. The third root is that of scientific thinking, which combines the first two streams of thought in recognizing that man indeed can study and conquer his environment, provide for his own needs, etc. The result of the combination of these three streams in a world of technology is that human existence is secularized or historicized. It comes to be determined, not by fate or by nature, but by time and history.[4]

We live in a world of history that has an open future.[5] This is a future in which Christians participate, not by trying to stop the mad rush of the world, but by rejoicing that man has been set free by God to shape his own destiny.[6] Their job is to be part of this world and this freedom, always seeking in the perspective of God's purpose for a world that can be truly human and truly responsible, to deny all man-made ideologies that would capture events and turn them into a closed system of ideas. The church is free to participate in history just because it believes that God is a God of history and that his plan and purpose for the world is at work in and through the plans and events that take place in our open-ended society.

2. Changing ideas of education

There is no way that the church can or should draw lines of separation between its own ideas of education and those of the society in which it lives.[7] In the first place, the church is a part of that society and world as seen by the fact that all of its educational thinking has been a process of interaction with the political and social context of its time.[8] In the second place, there is no difference in the process of education as such, whether it takes place in the school, church, home, or factory. In each case the process of education is one of actualizing and modifying the development of the total person in and through dialogical relationships.[9] The difference in Christian education is in terms of the perspective. Here Christ and his Spirit are the teachers who lead and instruct to maturity, and the educator accepts the position of cooperative partnership with the educated (see p. 23). In the last place, the major responsibility of the church in the field of education is not in the construction of elaborate educational systems of its own but in serving its Lord in the world as a leaven in the secular educational system. Thus Robert Lynn says in his book *Protestant Strategies in Education*, "Our first intent, therefore, is help the school be a school and not the frightened shadow of American society."[10] Christian education is participation in Christ's invitation to join in God's mission of restoring men to their true humanity. Such participation is meaningless, if not impossible, where it does not include relevant concern and action in terms of areas of neglect in the American school system.

The analyses of the present problems of the American school system are doubly fascinating to the Christian educator. Not only do they open up new ideas of the process of education, but also they provide a parable of the educational problems of the church. Like the church, the institution of American public education is about fifty years behind the times. It is so beset with the disease of "morphological fundamentalism" that it appears almost impossible to let ideas and up-to-date thinking change the outworn structures of organization.[11] Like the church, public education needs a revolutionary change of structure. Without a thoroughgoing reorganization from top to bottom, school systems like that of New York and of Chicago and those of smaller cities and towns will continue to "mis-educate" the poor and oppressed and lead the others to mediocrity regardless of additional money, teachers, and buildings. Thus the *Haryou Report* says that the key program for all educational reform for youth in Harlem is "a fundamental structural revision of the Harlem Schools. The total reorganization of the educational system is demanded by the findings of HARYOU's study of Harlem's schools."[12] The schools are being spurred on in their new ideas more by the race to the moon against Russia and the need for a passport to a college education than by a recognition of the cries for revolutionary reform that are coming from the social protest movements. Nevertheless, some exciting changes are being made possible by new investigations.

In recent years there has been a revival of interest in the field of education, for it has become not only the key to mobility and vocational success, but also the key to scientific and technological excellence. At the same time, new ideas in education have been coming forth from "university scholars, educational foundations (governmental and private), experimental psychologists and other social scientists, and imaginative schoolmen."[13] In short, history has caught up with educational thinking, and it is beginning again to experiment with the meaning of change and process. Pioneering is going on in the harnessing of technology to education, changing patterns of teaching, and investigating the process of learning and comprehension.[14]

Among these changes are three that are particularly relevant to our discussion of Christian education. One change is that educators are beginning to talk about *education for a world of change*. We live in a world of change where things happen so fast that it is not possible to give people a fund of knowledge that will be adequate for life in a technological world a few years hence. Thus education must help men to live with permanent change, help them to live in a "modern mobile world."[15] The use of technology, modern teaching aids, and the sciences of learning and motivation must help to speed up the educational process so that students are enabled to gain a wider knowledge of the world we live in, and a more detailed technical knowledge needed to live and work in any particular area of the modern world.

A second change is that educators are beginning to investigate *the structure of knowledge* and the way in which a student may come to grasp the fundamental manner in which things are related in a particular discipline so that learning can serve the student in the future. "Learning should not only take us somewhere; it should allow us later to go further more easily."[16] This type of learning, according to Bruner in his excellent book *The Process of Education*, consists of "learning initially not a skill but a general idea, which can then be used as a basis of recognizing subsequent problems as special cases of the idea originally mastered."[17] It makes it possible to teach the foundations of any subject to anybody at any age in some form. It involves learning to think intuitively (using "the intellectual technique of arriving at plausible but tentative formulations without going through the analytic steps by which such formulations would be found to be valid or invalid conclusions"). Such learning stresses interest in the material to be learned as the best stimulus for learning rather than outside motivation. Bruner's theory is still to be tested, but it provides valuable clues for our thinking about Christian education.[18]

A third change in educational discussion is the stress on *teaching as part of a production team*. In modern technological society much of the work is accomplished through production teams or task forces.[19] Each person plays his own role in the team and performs a function in working in a disciplined way toward the particular goal. Such teams in business, government, and industry are not permanent, but *ad hoc* groups formed for a particular function and disbanded or reorganized when that function is no longer useful. Examples of such teams would be a Presidential task force on poverty, an army task force in Vietnam, or a production team in a General Motors plant. In the area of education they can function in two important ways. (*a*) In terms of new teaching methods in which teachers are part of a functioning team so that each person provides a skill or function for the teaching of the particular discipline, which is being carried out by the whole team. This provides flexible use of skills and talents, and flexible organization of teaching teams that can be formed and re-formed according to specific tasks. (*b*) The other way production teams can function is in terms of the pupils themselves who may find new interest and motivation in learning as part of a problem-solving functional team that has a particular job to do as part of its learning experience.

3. Christian education in a changing world

Christian education today finds itself in the same predicament as public education. It too must be education in a world of change and process. It too must face the fact of "morphological fundamentalism" in churches, which makes the task of education for change difficult, if not impossible. While public education is spurred on by the "race to the moon," Christian education is being spurred on by "death of God" theology which strikes fear in the hearts of those who are afraid that people will find that he has been buried in the church for years. How can we make twentieth-century Christians for a world of change? We cannot. But we *can* participate in Christ's invitation to join God's mission of restoring men to their true humanity by trying to find how Christ is shaping the lives of men and equipping them for this mission in the world. As we try to listen to the Biblical message concerning the way God acts in the light of the events of our own time, a few tentative clues emerge concerning the kind of equipment and education we all need to serve in the world.

One clue is that we need *freedom and courage to live with questions* instead of answers. In a changing world, there are only changing answers. In fact, as Hans Hoekendijk writes in his book *The Church Inside Out,* there may be only questions and more questions.[20] A Christian needs freedom and openness to the future so that he can live with questions, ask questions, and participate in an open-ended world of history (see Part III). Another clue is that we need *an intuitive knowledge about the Christian faith* that will enable us to view the world in which we live with "eyes of faith." Viewing the world from the angle of our faith in God's activity in that world helps us to risk new decisions and insights that are called for by the "new occasions" of history. Such intuitive insight is a result of learning not just the facts and the history of the Christian faith but also the meaning of the Christian faith as lived out in a life of service. The context of such learning is the Christian community. This context should provide an opportunity for the Christian to make decisions and carry out actions not only in terms of analysis of rules already set down but also in terms of intuitive expression of the relationship of love and trust that he finds in that community (see Part II). A third clue is that we need to be able to *celebrate life* in relation to God and the world and our brothers. Such celebration would express the fact that we enjoy the world in which we live simply because it is God's world—a world where he makes himself known in the events of history, a world that finds its meaning and purpose in terms of his love for it (see Parts IV and V). In a world of change the process of Christian education must always be changing as well. But Christian education itself remains a gift of God's love offered by Christ to all men so that they may join him in his mission.

PART TWO

The Context of Christian Education—
A Witnessing Community

Deuteronomy 6:4–9, 20–25

"Hear, O Israel: The Lord our God is one Lord; and you shall love the Lord your God with all your heart, and with all your soul, and with all your might. And these words which I command you this day shall be upon your heart; and you shall teach them diligently to your children, and shall talk of them when you sit in your house, and when you walk by the way, and when you lie down, and when you rise. . . .

"When your son asks you in time to come, 'What is the meaning of the testimonies and the statutes and the ordinances which the Lord our God has commanded you?' then you shall say to your son, 'We were Pharaoh's slaves in Egypt; and the Lord brought us out of Egypt with a mighty hand; . . . and the Lord commanded us to do all these statutes, to fear the Lord our God, for our good always, that he might preserve us alive, as at this day.' "

The great commandment of Deut. 6:4–5 is a positive formulation of the first commandment (Deut. 5:7) and calls for unconditional and exclusive worship and service of the God who saved Israel. In v. 5, Deuteronomy uses one of his favorite sermonic expressions to declare that the people of Israel should love and serve God with their whole being even as God the Father has loved and saved them. Verses 4–9 form a confession of faith that is spelled out in a series of sermons on its meaning and implications for the life of Israel in the time of Deuteronomy in chs. 6 to 11.[1] Verses 20–25 use what is probably an old confessional formula recited at convenant renewal ceremonies to emphasize the way in which the Shema is to be taught to children (Deut. 6:21–23; 26:5–9; Josh. 24:2–13). They make it clear that God's commands are not a burden or punishment but an act of grace so that his people might receive the promised gifts of shalom.[2]

In presenting the great commandment in this fashion, Deuteronomy shows that the commands of God are not a known quantity that can be taught by rote, but are something learned by experience.[3] They are learned by participation in a witnessing community—a community such as Israel whose children participated in the history of God's salvation with their fathers, so that all might know that they had been delivered from bondage and were free to serve their one Lord. Today Christian education still takes place in a *witnessing community*—a community that knows and celebrates the story of God's salvation in words and actions. This story cannot be taught by rote. It is a story that can only be lived, and when it is lived in celebration of God's past, present, and future acts of deliverance, then the witness will be heard and lived by all those who share in God's promise of life (Acts 1:8).

NO EDUCATION
WITHOUT A WITNESSING COMMUNITY

1. The church in the world as the context of Christian education

CHRISTIAN EDUCATION is participation in Christ's invitation to all people to join in God's mission of restoring men to their true humanity. Christ himself carries out this work and is, therefore, the teacher. Through the power of the Spirit he extends this invitation, and he is continually at work carrying out God's purpose and plan for the world. However, as "participation" implies, the Christian educator is also involved in the action. For Christ allows him to participate with him in the work of extending the invitation (II Cor. 5:19–20). At the same time, the people who hear the invitation allow him to participate with them in both the hearing of the call and the response (II Cor. 1:24). The context of this participation is a witnessing community of Christians who participate with Christ in extending his invitation, and who participate with all men in hearing and responding.[1]

Webster's Dictionary tells us that the word "context" means the part of a passage "preceding or following a particular word or group of words and so intimately associated with them as to throw light upon their meaning."[2] This is the type of role that the community plays in Christian education. It is the part of the continual discourse between Christ and the world in which the invitation occurs and which helps to explain its meaning. Man needs such a context in order to grow in his understanding of Christ's call, because he has been created in interdependence (Gen. 1:27; 2:18). He finds his own humanity only as he is able to live in a relationship of love and obedience with God, and love and service with his brothers. He is able to grow in the "discipline and instruction of the Lord" only as he is related to others who are receiving the same nurture.[3]

A witnessing community is not necessarily any particular type of church. It is simply a gathering of people in the name of Jesus Christ (Matt. 18:20). They are a community because they are gathered together by his love and thus related to one another by their love for Christ. They are a witnessing community because the love of Christ is too wonderful not to be shared—shared in telling others the good news of God's love by words and actions of love and service. Such a community is like the community of Israel because it proclaims the mighty acts of God's deliverance and lives out that proclamation day by day (Deut. 6:21). However, it is different from Israel in that its witness is turned outward toward all the nations (Rom. 1:5). With the coming of the Messiah the people of God no longer wait for all nations to be drawn in to be united with them in the Holy City. Instead, they are sent out by Christ, following him to the end of the earth and witnessing to the message of his victory to all nations (Acts 1:8; Matt. 24:14). As Yves Congar puts it in his excellent book *The Wide World, My Parish:* "The Church's mission is as wide as the world. The Lord's followers will never come to an end of evangelizing man where he is found, beginning with themselves."[4] By their every action, those gathered in Christ's name become his witnesses, seeking always to point to him who is the true Faithful Witness (martyr) (Rev. 1:5).

A witnessing community always finds itself in the world.

It does not belong to the world, for it is *"set apart* for God, . . . in order to be again sent to the world" and owes its loyalty to Christ and his Kingdom (Phil. 3:20).[5] Yet it has to be a church in the world because that is where Christ is at work. That is where Christians respond to the invitation of Christ to join in God's mission, and that is where men live and where they need to be served. Such a community must be part of the whole world because its reason for being is to serve that whole as a light, as a leaven, as a part that is simply "added on" in order to represent the firstfruits of the redemption of the world so that all might see and rejoice (Matt. 5:14–16; Rom. 8:22–23).

For good or for ill it is the Christian community that is the context of Christian education. Often that context is weak and the invitation to join in God's work is not lived out. When this happens and the community is not a *witnessing* community, those who are being nurtured in the community receive "miseducation" or a gift of education that has already been turned into a stone (see Part I). This situation is a basic fact to which Christian educators frequently feel called to testify. Thus in 1862, Orestes Bronson wrote of Catholic education that it failed to produce "live men, active thinking men, great men" because the Catholic Church thought its duty was to take its stand for past civilization and resist all progress. In 1917, George A. Coe wrote that what the church *is* speaks louder than what it *says,* so that when there is no self-criticism and the church supports the *status quo* this is all that is learned. And in 1965, Robert Lynn wrote, "The present parlous state of Protestant education . . . is also a sign of a flabby church that has lost its way and forgotten its true vocation."[6]

2. *Christian education is missionary education*

Christian education is missionary education by definition. It is participation in Christ's invitation to join in

God's *mission* in the world. Its context is a witnessing, or *missionary,* community. Its job is to participate with Christ in equipping men for God's mission. The mission belongs to God and not to the church, because God is the one who does the sending. He sends his Son. He sends his Spirit. He sends his church into the world to witness to his actions of salvation, as a part of those actions. God's mission, his purpose and plan for the world, is that he "desires all men to be saved and to come to the knowledge of the truth" (I Tim. 2:4). God is at work restoring men to their true humanity by reconciling them to himself and to one another. Their true humanity can be seen in Christ's relationship of obedient service toward God and loving service toward man (Phil. 2:5–8). Man's true humanity and salvation consists of his wholeness and health of relationship with God, his neighbor, and himself, which can be seen in the creation of Adam and in the life, death, and resurrection of Jesus Christ. The signs that in Christ this mission to restore all creation to wholeness is being realized are Christ's actions of judgment, healing, and reconciliation in the New Testament and in our own lives (Matt. 11:1–6; Luke 4:18–19).[7]

The church is called by God to participate in his mission, and therefore, by its very nature, it is missionary.

It is thus of the very nature of the church that it has a mission to the whole world. That mission is our participation in the work of God which takes place between the coming of Jesus to inaugurate God's kingdom on earth and his coming again in glory to bring that kingdom to its consummation.[8]

When we use the words "mission" and "missionary" in this way, we are talking about God's saving action in the world, and our part in this action. We are not talking about what is commonly known as "missions." "Missions" (foreign or home missions) is a word derived from God's mission and refers simply to a particular development of the church's missionary concern since the beginning of the nineteenth century. In order to emphasize the work of the church in God's mission, the word "evangelism" is often used. This word also refers to the whole life of the church and means "the church's participation in the messianic work of Christ."[9] It is the way the church lives out the good news that in Christ all men have been reconciled as it waits for the final fulfillment of God's promise by proclaiming the gospel message, living that message in its community life, and making that message clear in acts of service. Evangelism is not proselytism or propaganda. Its purpose is not to make more church members or plant new churches. Nor is it to brainwash people into thinking and acting like itself.[10] Rather, its purpose is to join Christ in extending his invitation to all men to participate in God's plan of making men truly human.

It becomes clear then that there is little difference in meaning between such words as "witness," "mission," "evangelism." They all refer to the whole nature and function of the church as it participates in God's sending and saving work. *There is also little difference between the meaning of these words and Christian education, for Christian education refers to participation in the same mission of God.* John Calvin himself saw this close relationship, for in his book on the Christian ministry in the *Institutes of the Christian Religion,* he makes it clear that preaching, etc., is a part of God's plan of education.[11]

The difference between Christian education and mission is only one of perspective. A part of the church's participation in Christ's invitation is its role as the context of the missionary education. From the educational perspective, its job is to be the place where missionary education takes place, the place where Christ nurtures and equips his people for joining in God's mission of restoring men to their true humanity.

3. Pluralistic church structures and educational pluralism

A witnessing community is not necessarily any one particular type of church structure. The structure or organizational shape of the community has to vary according to the functions of the community and the needs that it serves. In society today there is great variety of social relationships. Such a variety is characterized by the word "pluralism."

> By pluralism we mean that in a relatively free society "any number can play" and large numbers do. That is, many religions, political forces, philosophies, clubs, patterns come into play and are employed by people to define themselves.[12]

This means that in a modern pluralistic society where there is no one pattern of social relationships, there should be a pluralism of church structures. Many people no longer find their center of interest where they reside. Often vocation, sports, arts, politics, etc., are their real points of concern. The residential congregation is no longer able to be the one pattern of church life if the communities of Christians are going to be gathered at the real points of interest, need, and action in society. Not only will there have to be a variety of types of congregations, but also all these communities will in themselves be constantly changing and reforming as the society around them changes.

Although it is clear that an infinite variety is possible in the structuring of witnessing communities, it is still possible to suggest several basic *types* of structure that correspond to the types of functions which they serve. One type is that of the *family structure*. This structure is basically residential in character and sees as its function the service of a particular segment of God's world in which it is located. Such a structure needs to be small enough so that solidarity in the service of the larger community is possible among those who feel called into a family of mutual trust and service. Another type is that of the *structure of permanent availability*. This structure is basically oriented around long-term tasks and seeks to make services available to people whenever and however they need them without necessarily trying to involve them in the life of that community. A third type is that of the *task force structure*. This structure is formed around a particular need or function and goes out of existence when that need has been accomplished.

An example of one larger framework that includes all three of these types is the East Harlem Protestant Parish in New York City.[13] This parish is a gathering of various types of witnessing communities in an interdependent *zonal structure* that "comprehends and integrates most of the various contexts around which the population is concentrated for the basic activities of local life."[14] The family-type structure is seen in the Church of the Ascension which serves the people who live directly around the church as a residential parish whose life is nurtured in witness and study for the sake of service to the community. The structure of permanent availability may be seen in the Central Services Center which provides casework, legal help, meeting rooms, etc., to the community and is available simply as people have need of the services rendered. The task force structure is illustrated by witnessing communities gathered to involve themselves in the problem of public education, or remedial reading, or narcotics, etc. While all the structures are in a state of constant change and growth, the task force structures are by far the most flexible and *ad hoc*. They are capable of disbanding or moving into a new area as their particular function is no longer needed.

With flexibility in structure, *membership in a witnessing community* becomes a matter of greater flexibility as well. Many of these groups would include non-Christians, because by nature they are task-oriented. Yet if they are to be witnessing communities, they must have some way by which they know themselves to be gathered in the name of Him in whose work they are engaged. There is no one way to do this, and there is no one way to solve the problem of membership, but there are a few guidelines that seem to fit this more flexible understanding of church structure.

First, membership in a witnessing community can only be based on the invitation to serve in the name of Christ —the invitation to join in God's mission. For membership in a witnessing community can set no boundaries in terms of privilege. Anyone, regardless of whether he is a member or not, should be welcome to join in all the activities of the community. Secondly, membership implies a willingness to be a part of a task-oriented team having solidarity with the others, even though people are able to perform tasks only according to their various abilities. Thirdly, membership is important because it gives each person an opportunity to say no or yes. This provides an opportunity for commitment to Christ and to his work for those who wish to make this response, and an opportunity to those who do not, to have their wishes respected. In terms of a particular witnessing community the members and non-members share fully in the service to the world, and the only distinction between them is in the nature of their commitment. The members of a witnessing community are committed to follow Christ wherever he leads, both in this particular group and other groups with which they will share for different functions. For in joining any one witnessing community, they have become members of Christ's church universal, and their commitment does not end when a particular group is disbanded or changed. The non-members are committed to a particular function, such as better housing or Bible study, and feel no commitment beyond the immediate purpose of the group. Fourthly, discipline in such witnessing communities should grow out of the particular needs of that group which will equip it to do its task.

It is obvious that the educational task in a variety of such forms must take *a variety of shapes*. Education in a family-type church is not the same as in an *ad hoc* structure serving alcoholics. The nurture takes place in the context of the communities themselves, and its shape changes accordingly. However, regardless of the type of witnessing community, one principle is clear—education and nurture have to take place "on the job." The way people are equipped for Christ's mission in the world is by being involved in that mission. They learn to celebrate what Christ has done and is doing among them by celebrating with others who have been granted the "eyes of faith" to see God's actions in the Bible and in the world of today.[15] They learn to serve Christ in the world by participating with others in service and being helped to be able to serve by the love and concern and trust of those around them. The witnessing community is the context of Christian education, and where it is involved in mission, education will also take place in mission and be missionary education.

4

EDUCATION IN A "FAMILY OF GOD"
AS A WITNESSING COMMUNITY

1. The "family of God" in the New Testament

IN A PLURALISTIC SOCIETY where there are many social groupings, there is no longer any one normative type of congregation. The family congregational structure is just one among other types and is suited to a ministry that is basically residential in character as it serves a particular segment of God's world in which it is located. The word "family" should not mislead people into thinking that it is a congregation exclusively devoted to families or to the private sector as over against the public sector of life. For the congregation may or may not serve family units. It will serve whoever dwells in its residential area, whether in families or not. It will serve all the contexts, private and public, around which a residentially based population is concentrated for its basic activities. It is called a family structure because *it is a family*—men and women and children of all ages, races, sexes, classes, joined together as one "family of God" in Jesus Christ.

In the New Testament the word "house" (*oikos*) plays a prominent place in the understanding of the way God gathered his people into congregations. This word, which is important and basic in any language, is applied to the congregation as a "household or family of God." In the Old Testament, house or household (*bayith*) had the meaning of the covenant people of God, and the place where they gathered for worship.[1] God was related to his house (Israel) in terms of owning it and ruling it and dwelling in its midst. In the New Testament the church was understood as "an eschatological gathering of God's people into his household" or family. The term "household of God" appears only three times in the New Testament (Eph. 2:19; I Peter 4:17; I Tim. 3:15). But the family imagery is used again and again to describe the relationships within the church as those of a household or family. Paul speaks of the necessity of doing good to "those who are of the household of faith" in Gal. 6:10, and of his work as one who nurtured the church like a father in I Thess. 2:11–12: "For you know how, like a father with his children, we exhorted each one of you and encouraged you and charged you to lead a life worthy of God, who calls you into his own kingdom and glory." There are also references to members of the congregation as a house of God in the sense of being a place where God dwells, like the Temple of the Old Testament (I Cor. 3:16; 6:19).

Other words from the same root as *oikos* are also important in the New Testament language. Thus *oikonomia* is the way the householder manages and orders his house and is used to refer to God's plan or economy (Eph. 1:10; 3:9). The word *oikoumenē* refers to the inhabited world and thus to all mankind. The word *oikodomē* means the act of building up the house and is used to refer to edification, improvement, strengthening (the Christian education) of the household of God (Eph. 4:29; I Cor. 14:4–5). In I Cor. 10:23, Paul states that " 'all things are lawful,' but not all things build up [edify]." He considers his task as an apostle that of building up or edifying the church (I Cor. 3:5 f.). He urges all members of the church to continue in mutual edification of one another (I Thess. 5:11) by giving men advice concerning edification in daily ethical matters (I Cor. 10:23) and in worship (I Cor., ch. 14).[2]

When we look at the New Testament references to find

out what sort of people were in the "families of God" we find that they were not restricted in any sense to the immediate family of one individual. There was no one particular pattern of who would be in the household of God, because anyone was welcomed into God's family regardless of walk of life. Therefore, the "household of God" varied in its makeup according to each circumstance. In general it appears to have met in someone's house (Rom. 16:3–5; Acts 16:14–15). A household in the Old and New Testament times was very unlike the small nuclear family as it is seen in American society. It was an extended family that included relatives, servants, slaves. When a "household of God" met for meals and celebration of the Lord's Supper in the residence of such a family, it was merely extended further to include as many other people as the house could hold (I Cor. 11:17–26).[3] The "house tables," or lists of ethical instructions to the members of the household of God, indicate that "the discipline and instruction of the Lord," when it occurred in the context of the family, included all ages and groups of people. Simply following the secular structures of the society in which they lived, the writers gave advice to husbands, wives, parents, children, slaves, and masters (Col. 3:18 to 4:1; Eph. 5:21 to 6:9). Thus we can conclude that a household or family of God was simply a small gathering of Christians who knew themselves to be united across all distinctions of class and race by the love of Christ (Gal. 3:27–28).

2. The "family of God" distinguished from the modern nuclear family

In the New Testament this *oikos,* or house, represented the whole of society because this was the way people gathered in that society, through extended family units. Therefore, the concept of "household of God," referring to God's gathering of his people into his household or community, coincided with the household structure of society at that time and was the only form necessary in order to be a church in the whole of society. However, today we are in a different situation. Although the family-type witnessing community has a structural similarity to the New Testament *oikos,* it is not able adequately to represent the concept of God's household that is part of all of society. Thus in addition to the family-type witnessing community that has structural similarity to the *oikos,* we need to have many other complementary and even contradictory structures that enable the church to be God's household in the other sectors of society, such as business, politics, and leisure time.

In a brief look at the development of church structures, we can see the way they have varied according to the social patterns of the times, and we can also see why we need to find new varieties of structures today. In a time when society hardly resembles the sixteenth century, American church structures are still dominated by the "myth" that the family and its corollary, the local parish church, are as important and relevant structures in society as they were in the time of the Reformation. In the period of the Middle Ages the churches gradually became large congregations of individuals whose home life was substantially secular and without Christian ritual.[4] By 1500 the idea of family had begun to change as greater security and the extension of education contributed to the evolution of the family as the arena for social living. It was this newly emerging family pattern of life that became the basis of the reformation of the church. "Worship life now drew support from each household in which the head of the home daily led the members in acts of worship and in instruction of Christian beliefs. The home became the basis of the 'new community' which gathered on Sunday to praise God."[5] In fact, Luther recommended the establishment of house churches for those who "mean to be real Christians and profess the Gospel with hand and mouth."[6]

With the advent of the industrial revolution, a new

group of people entered the social scheme who had no relevance to the pattern of church life. Although the church could adjust its message, which was dominated by the virtues of rural life, to the family life of merchants and manufacturers, it found that it had little or nothing to say to the city proletariat. Its family structure was so bound up with the teachings of the Reformers that it was blind to the fact that again the "household" had to be formed to meet the new kind of culture emerging in crowded, poverty-stricken slums. In spite of the work of John Wesley and other Reformers who recognized that the church had to find new ways of ministry through organization in small house meetings, fighting the social and economic conditions of the proletariat, and preaching with new power, the Protestant Church as a whole became identified with the middle-class family structure.[7]

The irony of this is not only that lack of flexible structures made the church irrelevant to large segments of industrial society but also that it continues to make it largely irrelevant even to modern middle-class society. The modern nuclear family of today has very little resemblance to the family of the time of the New Testament or of the Reformation. According to Talcott Parsons, the word "family" in the United States refers only to the conjugal unit and not to relatives. People belong only to two family units: the unit of orientation and the unit of procreation. It is the conjugal family that is the normal household unit, and isolation as a unit is its most dominant feature. Status and economic support are derived from employment, and not from kin.[8] The nuclear unit lasts only as long as it performs one or both of its two basic functions of socialization of the children to be members of society and stabilization of the adult person in the population of the society.[9] The modern nuclear family is small because it must be mobile, constantly moving according to the family's social mobility and the parents' particular occupational base. Such a family is still the locus of value behavior in American society, but it has influence only in the private sector of life and in turn is influenced by and dependent upon public institutions such as politics, economics, and class. The church, in the name of being a family church, has largely ministered to the family by simply becoming an adjunct to it and abdicating its relationship to the public or community sector of life.[10]

Today no church structure, including that of the family type, should be completely shaped as an extension of the modern nuclear family. Society today is made up of many other structures that give meaning to life, and to identify with this form is to place the church in captivity to the private sector of life. This was not true in the time of the Reformation, because the meaningful unit of society was the family, and the church found its best form in that locus. However, the "family of God" structure as one among many types of structures can be a gathering of God's people into *his* household, regardless of whether the people themselves are in families. The family-type structure of a witnessing community is a household in this sense that it recognizes its basic purpose as the gathering of men, women, and children in the service of a particular residential area. Roman Catholic theology, following the lead of Thomas Aquinas, has asserted that the parish is like a family and not like a city (Pope Pius XI, 1923). Yves Congar, in his article *Mission de la Paroisse,* distinguishes two basic social groupings as *family* and *civitas* and says that the family corresponds to the parish and the city to the diocese.[11] The family of God receives its particular name from the fact that its emphasis is upon the family-type function of mutual solidarity and sympathy among all its members regardless of their status in life or ability to serve. Other structures are shaped by their emphasis on the different functions that they perform for the *civitas.*[12]

3. Characteristics of a family-type structure

What are the specific characteristics of a family-type church? It shares certain basic characteristics with all the forms of witnessing community: solidarity in service to the world; study of Scripture as the basis of understanding God's mighty acts and his mission in the world; sacramental celebration with Christ as he nurtures and sustains them to serve in his name (Acts 2:42).[13] But the main characteristic of a family-type church is that it be a family; that it have the kind of mutual sympathy, trust, and forgiveness among its members that will enable them to know, perhaps for the first time, what it is like to be in a family where a person is loved in spite of all his weaknesses and faults, loved just because he is a brother in Christ. The effect that one such family-type church had on a teen-age boy who had been deserted by his parents at age thirteen was to cause him to say that the reason he was joining the church was that the "church is the only place I ever knew people who help you and don't take advantage of you. I know I can count on the church and want to be a part of it." And it caused another teen-age boy to say: "I spent sixteen years doing nothing, just goofing off. Then I helped with the kids in vacation church school and found out what fun it was to teach them. Now I work with the children, and this makes me want to do better in school."

The characteristic of the family-type community is that it *functions like a family* where love and trust is found. All the people related to the church are treated as children; that is, they are loved and helped. They are never rejected because they go to jail or wear the wrong color tie or talk too much; they are helped to help one another, to play with one another, to work with one another, to criticize one another. In short, they are *at home*. Of course, all types of witnessing communities need mutual solidarity and trust, but the others are focused on the function that they perform and thus may in fact exclude those unable to fulfill that function. The family relationship is not sentimental. It involves the kind of *sympathy* that comes from knowing that no matter how weak another person is, you do not need to stoop down to help him, because your weaknesses have put you there alongside of him already. Perhaps this is why Peter became such a good leader of the church. He never was able to look down on any man but could only stand with men in sympathy, knowing that he himself had denied Christ three times. It implies a *small enough group* where there can be face-to-face contact between all the members so that they can really share their lives and concerns together.

The role of the family-type witnessing community as the context of Christian education is that everything it does as a family is part of the *process of nurture* of all the members. Whether or not it has a Sunday school is not even important if it is small enough so that it is able to include the children in the worship, work, and play of the total witnessing community. They will learn by participation in the family life the same way children learn at home, and concerned adults will find various ways to teach the children by study, action, drama, music, etc., which will not necessarily take place in a formal Sunday school situation. This was the way nurture took place in the early church. There is no evidence in the early catechisms from the end of the second century that baptized children ever received formal instruction. Rather, they learned with their parents, attending the liturgy of the church where they were allowed to shout *"Kyrie"* at the appropriate moments.

Even the adult catechumens learned to be Christians by participation in the life of the church over a three-year period before the forty days of intensive doctrinal instruction concerning the meaning of the Sacraments before their Baptism. After a preliminary inquiry as to the motive for joining the church and instruction into the meaning of the Christian faith, the catechumens were admitted as Christians to the fellowship so that they could be instructed by participating in the service of the Word, and by special classes. Then after two to three years, the catechumens were examined to see if they were living a Christian life, and were admitted to a period of intensive instruction concerning the meaning of the Sacraments as preparation for Baptism. Lewis Sherrill states that the function of "the catechumenate was that of gradually inducting adults into the Christian community."[14] And following Baptism, they continued to be instructed in sacramental life in recognition that nurture continues to take place after Baptism and for the whole rest of the Christian life.

The *shape* of this family life is basically matriarchal.[15] It is not matriarchal in the sense that it involves only women or mothers, but in the sense that the leadership skills needed to nurture a family-type congregation are similar to those needed by a mother in caring for her own family. The family life is nurtured by those who are willing to "keep the home fires burning," by those who are willing to be concerned with the day-to-day life and problems of people in such a way that they are helped to be able to participate in Christ's mission in the world.

It should be clear from this description of the family type of witnessing community that most modern residential congregations do not fit in this category. This is because they have just grown, like Topsy, never changing their structures, just adding things on as they followed the nuclear family into its private world and tried to provide for all its mobile and varied needs while still maintaining some semblance of being a folksy family church. In a great number of cases such congregations are much too large to be family churches even if many families participate in their programs. They need to rethink their structures, perhaps shifting to other types, or at least becoming a collection of ministries or communities with various functions. Such large urban and suburban churches provide many services that could be rendered by structures of permanent availability, such as great preachers, magnificent choirs, dynamic youth groups, extensive counseling services, marriages, funerals. They also find in their community many opportunities for the gathering of small task force structures that could address themselves over a longer or shorter period of time to local political structures, public education, fair housing, civil rights, ministry to businessmen, study of the Bible, etc. Many families might find exciting possibilities for involvement and nurture if they were allowed to form into small family-type congregations of fifty to a hundred members. In addition to breaking down their own structures into various functional units that could be linked together and coordinated with a central budget and opportunities for great rallies and festivals, the churches could also profitably consider viewing their segment of the city as a zone and joining with other church groups in agreeing to offer different services with different types of groups, so that they could be united in serving their community by offering complementary rather than competing programs.

4. The nurturing role of the minister in a matriarchal structure

Hans Hoekendijk has recently raised a question concerning whether it is any longer possible for a man to be a minister of a family-type congregation because of its matriarchal character.[16] For the basic role of a minister in such a congregation is to participate with Christ and with his congregation in helping all the "children" of the family to grow in the "discipline and instruction of the Lord" (Eph. 6:4; I Thess. 2:11). It has long since been recognized that such an occupation of equipping the saints so that they may go forth to "win the battles" calls for a certain amount of feminine characteristics. Men who are ministers tend to possess a high degree of these characteristics.

In such a family-type community the minister can stop worrying about whether he should be a pastoral director, a business administrator, an orator, an enabler, an educator, a theological reflector, or what. He has to be a "mother." He has to tend the house, be a jack-of-all-trades, ready to do anything at all times, ready to love the children of God so much that he loves them into loving others. Indeed, like any mother, he may find that an emergency or a particular need calls him to go out and be the bread-winner on the front line of life, but even when this happens, and he is leading the troops into battle or raising funds to feed the troops, his work at home is never done and he must be binding the wounds and keeping up everyone's spirits. This is a serious job, a job in which the minister's feeling for the wholeness and health of the entire family is a key to the way in which that family is nurtured and strengthened by Christ's love.

It should be made clear here that I am not speaking of the church as the bride of Christ. Rather, I am using the analogy of the church as the body of Christ. Christ is its head, and the people, the members of the body (I Cor. 12:12–31). The best comparison to the role of the minister in this body is the role of the wife in a family. He functions not as the head but as the *heart* of the family-type congregation, constantly working to be an instrument of Christ's love in the nurture and growth of the whole body. This function can be performed well by either men or women. The important thing is not the sex of the minister, but whether the minister has the talents and concern for being the heart of a family structure. Those who do not face the importance of this role frequently find their ministry in a family-type congregation stunted by a need to justify its validity by more typically male roles of vigorous organizational and administrative plans, fine pub-

lic speaking, militant social action, individual pastoral
counseling, and the like. The fact is that all these things
are important skills in the life of the church, but the one
most needed in a family-type congregation is that of being
a "mother."[17]

Not only is the minister's role in such a family fairly
clear, but so also is his relationship to the laity. When he
is working with a smaller congregation helping them to
perform their ministry in the world, he has no way of
hiding from mutual criticism. They know all about him,
including many things that he does wrong. Nor can he
escape into administration, speechmaking, etc., because
there is a very limited amount of this which needs to be
done in such a group. Rather, his major task is to participate with all the members of the church in their education
and nurture, recognizing that his role as "mother" is not
one of superiority but one of function. Like any mother,
he serves the family. Like any mother, he does not feel
superior to the children, but rather spends all his time and
energy helping them to grow up to be better and wiser and
more loving than himself. If such a group is small enough,
it may not need a paid minister, in which case he might
have a secular job as well. Or if arrangements can be made
for the administration of the Sacraments through some
other church community or if permission is granted to
administer them without ordained clergy, the leader of
such a group could be a layman, or even a *real mother*
who has gifts in the nurturing of others. But in a family-
type structure there is a clear need for someone or a group
who has the function of "equipping the saints" and caring
for the health of the whole family.

5. The nurturing role of the whole congregation in a matriarchal structure

In a family-type witnessing congregation, all age groups,
types, and classes of people are included. The only limita-
tion on who is a part of such a congregation is the nature

of the population living in its particular residential community. Because all ages are included in the family, all ages should be included in the various types of nurturing activities. Thought has to be given to how adults as well as children and youth may participate in Christ's invitation to join in God's mission. The lists of ethical duties, or "house tables," of the New Testament indicate that they were clear that all groups, including slaves, needed to be included in nurture and advice (Col. 3:18 to 4:1; Eph. 5:21 to 6:9). As a family, all the groups participate in the ongoing life of worship, study, and service, and teach one another by the things that they do. Also, as a family they can all participate in helping to teach one another. This concern for one another and for mutual building up or edification (*oikodomē*) of the household of God is seen in the writings of the New Testament. Here Paul urges the churches to "instruct one another"; to "bear one another's burdens"; to be "subject to one another." (Rom. 15:14; Gal. 6:2; Eph. 5:21.) And I Peter speaks of practicing "hospitality ungrudgingly to one another."[18]

The process of teaching is that each person uses his talents to teach someone else. Even the little children can teach one another and their parents by putting on plays, singing songs, and doing projects. As the children get older, they not only teach one another by group programs, but they can learn to be teacher assistants to children younger than themselves. The youth can also teach as well as be taught and are able to teach one another better than many adults, to say nothing of being able to teach adults a thing or two in Bible study and other discussion groups.[19] Adults can teach one another in small Bible study groups by their own study and discussion, and can also do a good job of teaching the minister if he is willing to participate with them instead of lecturing. The most important part of this "each one teach one" approach is not only that it gives each person a chance to participate with Christ in the nurture of himself and of his brothers, but also that it provides in-service training in maturity (Eph. 4:1–16). Everyone in the family is helped to serve someone else. The requirement of being mature enough to serve extends only as far as whether they are willing to serve in some way. The whole congregation thus lives in a style of life where everyone knows he is there to serve someone else, so that growth in maturity and service becomes "doing what comes naturally."

6. Let the family church be the family church

The "family of God" as a witnessing community is only one type of structure among others. It should be the structure of a church only if that is the most relevant structure in terms of the people of the witnessing community and of the functions it needs to perform as part of Christ's work in the world. A church that really wants to have this type of structure should assess whether it can best serve the unmet needs of its community in this way. It should ask itself if its community is truly residential in the sense that the people actually *live* where they reside. For instance, business executives would be better served by a community that is concerned with their major interest— business. On the other hand, a slum community is more likely to be truly residential in that the people who sleep there find their life meaning in the same community. Large numbers are unemployed and never leave the ghetto at all, while many others have such poor jobs that they only really live when they are "at home" in the ghetto.[20] If the community is not residential in this sense, the church should ask itself what variety of forms might help it to be where people *are,* besides that of a family-type structure.

Secondly, it should ask itself if it is able to gather in face-to-face relationships where the community is small enough so that mutual help and criticism are possible. If it is too large, which is often the case, it should ask itself if the church should be broken down into a variety of structures, possibly with a "cathedral" type church as the central gathering point of the smaller churches. Thirdly, a church should ask itself if it is able to be really inclusive. One of the advantages of a family-type congregation is that it can include all types of people, classes, and races, and is especially helpful in including outcasts and misfits of society in a family of mutual concern. It may be that a family type that has only one type and class of people in it had better be a task force community trying to fight against housing zones and discrimination. At any rate, a witnessing community made up of all one type of person, be they all narcotics addicts or all old ladies or all middle-class families, is better suited to a task force structure so that their reason for being together becomes focused in a problem or function and not on the fact of their cultural homogeneity. Fourthly, the minister or leader of a family-type community should ask himself if he really wants to be in this "mother" role of equipping the saints. If he does not, there are many other types of ministry available in other forms of witnessing congregations. For those congregations that really seek by their structure to be a "family of God," there will be ever new opportunities to learn of the ways in which Christ is at work in their midst to equip men for his work in the world.

EDUCATION IN OTHER FORMS
OF WITNESSING COMMUNITIES

1. Pluralistic social structures and other forms of witness-
ing communities

IN THE PLURALIST SOCIETY in which we live "any number can play" and the variety of structures in which they
"play" are characterized by differentiation, concentration,
and mobility. The church that serves such a world must
therefore take shape around these characteristics.[1] Its ministry can take shape in terms of differentiation and concentration if it is willing to allow for a variety of witnessing
communities entirely concentrated and specialized in one
particular arena of society. Its ministry can take shape in
terms of mobility if it allows communities to be constantly
changing in their shape and focus according to the task of
ministry to which Christ has called them and if it provides
freedom for people to move from group to group. The
family-type witnessing community must take all these
factors into account, and, above all, it must recognize
that it is not doing the whole job. Although it does concentrate on one particular residential area, its main role
in relation to these forces in society is to help people to
live with them creatively and to seek to bring wholeness to
men's lives at points where the pressures of such a society
cause lack of identity and loss of community.

On the other hand, the other two basic types of witnessing communities—structures of permanent availability,

and task force structures—take their shapes from these characteristics of modern technological society. A *task force community* concentrates on one particular task that needs to be done. It is *ad hoc,* to this job, in a more intense way than the other two structural types because it comes into being only for the purpose of doing a certain job and stops or is changed in orientation when the job is finished. A task force community is mobile because it always is able to change and move and to go where the action is. It is differentiated because it recognizes the need for an endless variety of task-oriented groups involved in Christ's mission in the world. The structures of permanent availability are designed to recognize the need for differentiation by providing certain permanent services to a society that itself is highly concentrated and yet highly mobile in an urban setting.

Such an attempt to view the structures of a witnessing community from the point of view of the way people gather for their functional service to the world tries to make clear that structure is not a static concept, but a concept of social process and change. The typology itself (structures typed according to family, task force, permanent availability) does not imply that these are fixed forms, but that this is one way of talking about the forms of witnessing community that are never strictly according to type, but are always changing in structure. "Structure is not a fixed pattern, a thing we can objectify; structure is always a moment in the process of destructuration and restructuration. It provides a group with enough identifiable form to be present in time. And therefore the structure is always necessarily an *ad hoc* structure."[2]

Understanding *structure as social process* enables us to find a completely different frame of reference for understanding the social expressions of the church from that of church sociologists of an earlier generation, such as Ernst Troeltsch. This typology distinguishes between church, sect, and "mysticism." It is mainly based on a historical study of the origin of such groups and assumes that the underlying social morphologies are, more or less, static. Such typologies, in addition to ignoring the fact that social structures are formed by social participation and thus are always part of the historical process, help to contribute to the "morphological fundamentalism" of denominational church structures. For, viewed in this static way, structures never change and tend to become accepted as sacred, God-given forms. Yet in a secular and historicized world, all structures and institutions are in process, and those which are not, such as denominational church structures, are obsolete.[3]

Although we can distinguish structures in terms of function, care should be taken not to assume that the structures themselves are static. Everything about these functional types of structures of witnessing communities is fluid except that they are "witnessing communities," communities gathered together by Christ, that they might be equipped to join in God's mission of restoring men to their true humanity. (a) They are fluid because the membership of the groups is always changing. People are free to belong to one or more groups at the same time, and to move from one group to the other. The various communities may or may not be linked together in a common zonal or overall structure. (b) They are fluid in that they do not all possess, all the time, all the basic characteristics of a witnessing community. A group may not have sacramental celebration with Christ, or it may not have common Bible study and reflection. Members of the group may feel that this is not possible because of the presence of so many non-Christians who are sharing in the common serving function. Or the members may be part of another fellowship that sustains them through worship and Bible study. Another group may be devoted mainly to Bible study, with the understanding that for that particular period of time this *is* their task so that the members of the group can provide deepening insights into the meaning of Christ's invitation as it relates to their day-to-day life. (*c*) The structures are fluid in terms of leadership, having a variety of trained team ministries whose training and relation to the group are conditioned by the group's ability and by its job. As George Casalis has put it, the "church reduced to its simplest expression" is a church where "the God of Jesus Christ and the world are taken seriously."[4] (*d*) The structure of a witnessing community is fluid just because it takes God's mission seriously and places itself at the disposal of Christ as he carries out this mission of reconciliation in the world. Thus its form follows the function that Christ gives it as part of his work in the world.

2. *Structures of permanent availability*

Siegfried von Kortzfleisch, who originated the idea of church structures of permanent availability, said that all that was needed for such a structure was a place and a man or a team.[5] Normally a "place" is needed because of the nature of the structure's function. It is to be permanently available so that people are able to avail themselves of the function. Thus an emergency telephone service for people contemplating suicide needs at least a telephone booth and a permanent number. A structure providing services of worship at noonday in a downtown business district needs a readily accessible meeting room suitable to such a service. A lay training academy, providing opportunities for dialogue concerning the meaning of the Christian faith in the modern world, needs a place to gather for such a discussion that is both easily accessible and also somewhat removed from daily distractions.

A "man" is needed in a structure of permanent availability to carry out the service offered. Yet I suspect that in most cases more than one man is needed, for if such a service is to be rendered over a long period of time on a stable basis so that it is well known to the public who might wish to use it, a team needs to be formed to render the service. With a team, continuity is preserved even if a particular person decides to leave the team for some other form of service. At the same time, a team will provide an opportunity for mutual solidarity and ministry, which is able to support those who are serving the world. Sometimes this is a group or a staff working as a team ministry in one location. Other times it is a group ministry of those working together in witnessing communities that are geographically close or functionally similar.[6] Sometimes this team is a permanent order such as the French Protestant community known as Taizé, which has its own disciplined life which equips it to provide a ministry of service to a particular community. Sometimes it is a disciplined community such as the Church of the Saviour in Washington, D.C., which renews its vows yearly as it strives to strengthen its membership in the ministry of coffeehouse, art shop, retreat, and rehabilitation center.[7]

In this type of structure the witnessing community is the team that gathers to render the service to the public at large. It does not seek to gather into the community those whom it serves. Rather, it offers its service as one it considers valuable in itself with no strings attached. When the need arises to refer people to a continuing Christian community, this should be done through interrelationships with family and task force structures and not by adding on to their own structure. This is because a structure of permanent availability will very easily betray its own calling by becoming a means of proselytism unless those doing the service are constantly aware of this danger. Thus, people who come to a particular place to get help with their personal problems and find themselves having to pay the price of being helped by attending some church are not slow to realize that there *are* "strings attached" to a supposedly free counseling service. Such a structure allows people in an anonymous world to remain anonymous if they so desire, and to receive the service offered without threatening to enfold them into the bosom of an unwanted fellowship. A cathedral-type church that provides opportunities for meditation and worship to all who enter should be willing to do just that, without feeling the need to shake each person's hand and make him sign the visitors' book.

In order to see how one witnessing community might function as an institution of permanent availability, let us look at Judson Memorial Church in Greenwich Village, New York City.[8] With the leadership of Robert Spike from 1950 to 1956 and of Howard Moody from 1956 to the present, this church has become a center of ministry to the people and events of Greenwich Village. This, of course, would lead us to think that it is a family-type church. But it is not. It is nonresidential in membership, drawing members from all over New York City who share an interest in its kind of program. The members of the congregation are largely middle-class intellectuals attracted by the intellectual integrity of the ministry and by an opportunity to share in developing new forms of ministry and witness.[9] The ministry of the church is to the youth and especially to the artists who live or congregate in the surrounding community. The church building is in constant use for productions involving drama, dance, art, and music. It provides a gathering place and forum for all manner of discussions and debates. It seeks to defend the right of the Village to be the Village through involvement in city politics. Yet the majority of the artists whom the church serves are not members and do not intend to become members.

According to any traditional morphological description, Judson Memorial Church is very ambiguous. It is a "church type" in being geographically based and sociologically inclusive. It is a "mystical type" in emphasizing the priority of the individual's faith reflecting its Baptist

heritage.[10] Yet from the point of view of functional structures, Judson Memorial Church is a good example of a
structure of permanent availability as it exists in real life,
including many elements that are in a state of fluidity and
change. The service it renders without strings attached is
the service of a gathering place for youth, artists, and the
socially concerned in the Village community. The ministering team is the membership of middle-class intellectuals
who enjoy serving in such a situation and spend a great
deal of time trying to understand how to make their church
really open and available to its world.[11] Membership in
such a church simply means joining the ministering team,
and it is not particularly relevant to the majority of those
who are served, as is indicated by the present discussions
in Judson concerning whether to have membership at all.
Worship tends to be relevant to the ministering team only,
but is a means of continual equipment and nurture for the
team. Thus the congregation of the church provides an
institution of permanent availability for the community of
Greenwich Village.

3. Task force structures

Unlike structures of permanent availability, task force
structures have no particular need of a "place." They
may or may not have a permanent gathering place according to the function that they perform. Their basic concern
is toward a problem, and all their energies focus on the
problem, so that most of their time is spent not in maintaining a building but in being involved in their task in
the world. A task force that is running a teen-age soda
fountain as a ministry to youth would have a storefront to
run the store, but a task force group involved in changing
the school zoning lines in a fight for quality integrated education might meet in a borrowed office, in someone's
home, on the steps of city hall, or in the bar around the
corner from the school board headquarters.

Task force structures always need more than one man. They need a witnessing community, a team of men and women and, sometimes, children who are willing to work for the cause. They have need of experts to help in their task who may be outside consultants, temporarily aiding in a particular job, or may be paid or volunteer resource members who are experts in community organization, race relations, city parks, theology, etc. With the help of the resource people, the whole team engages in continual self-education and preparation by means of dialogue concerning their understanding of the way God is at work in the world and the "happenings of God" that they see around them. Thus a remedial reading team will include people trained in teaching reading, in relations with the local school, in understanding youth and parents of a particular community, etc. A task force working with problems of addiction will include a psychiatrist, a social worker, a hospital liaison, a lawyer, a minister, a manual training expert, etc. A group of eight clergymen taking secular jobs in the city life of Philadelphia "to observe what God is doing through the laity and seek to discern in that *secular situation* the nature of Christian obedience and presence" will have to find experts in government, city planning, etc., in order to carry out their task.[12]

Such task forces are very similar in structure to what Kimball and McClellan call a "production team."[13] Such teams in business, government, and industry gather together the people needed to do a particular job and let them function as a team as long as those particular production and personnel arrangements are useful. In the same way, task forces are normally not of very long duration. They should be constantly aware of the necessity to be "wise as the serpents" of industry and to disband when someone else begins to do their work in a better way or when the task is done. Although they may continue for a number of years, there should be an evaluation at least once every year concerning whether they are still needed and in what form.

The groups should view their job as that of being a leaven in society to try to point the way to the eradication of points of injustice and inhumanity. Once they are able to help society to take over a particular function, they should disband or at least retain a role only of watchdog, concerned with helping the government or community organization that has taken over function with real integrity. Thus a narcotics committee that gets the government to take on the major job of the rehabilitation of addicts may become part of the governmental project or may redefine its role. A civil rights group that fosters the growth of a stronger and larger chapter of CORE in its community might decide to disband and become part of that group. On the other hand, a group that has been working with the housing and buildings department may decide that it can best serve the cause of better housing by disassociating itself from the governmental agency and becoming an independent pressure group for change. A house Bible study group should disband at least once a year, even if it begins again in another form, to keep its membership from becoming ingrown.

The size of a task force group is also determined by its function. Normally it will be small enough so that the members can work together on a particular project. But it might number a hundred or more if it seeks to mobilize people in a wider area to press for social change. Also the size will never be exact because the witnessing community will always include many people who work with it on a temporary or on a less intensive basis. A group devoted to Bible study or to beautification of a public park might be small, whereas a group devoted to changing the Constitution of the United States or subverting the structure of American church life might be nationwide in scope.

Regardless of the type of task force, the structure will

need to be in constant change as it works in a constantly changing world. Even its disciplines or style of life will be changing as they help equip the community for its particular task.[14] Education in such a context will be a most exciting adventure in dialogue and reflection on the way Christ is extending his invitation to join in God's mission at a particular hour, in a particular place, and in a particular year.

4. Permanent availability and task force structures as the context of education

Because the structures of the witnessing communities are fluid, there is no way of pinpointing the educational process in each type of community. In every case, the *structure* of the education will be that of the dialogue between God and his world as it is heard and celebrated in the life of the witnessing community. The *method* of education will be that of participation in the total life and work of the community as the power of Christ shapes it for mission. The *purpose* of the education will be celebration as men and women find freedom from themselves and from every man-made ideology to participate in God's actions of liberation (Luke 4:18–19). However, the *context* of the education, the shape of the witnessing community where the education takes place, will determine the particular type of educational task that is performed. Thus the education will follow the function of the group.

It is difficult to give examples of the way in which the context of task force or permanent availability structures determine the particular type of educational task. Concrete educational plans can evolve only "in situation." Education has to take place in involvement. The planning of educational programs must also take place in involvement. It must take place in the situation where men and women are participating in a dialogue between what the gospel says and what is happening in the part of the world where they are called to serve.[15] At best, examples can serve only as parables of the way that particular communities have found of participating with Christ in extending the invitation to join in God's mission. And it is difficult to give even hints when the experience of concrete situations is not firsthand. However, such hints are necessary here in order to give a perspective on how a variety of structures give rise to a variety of educational tasks.

The distinctive characteristic of structures of permanent availability is that they provide services that are needed in a modern mobile society. These services are made available whenever and however people need them without any attempt to involve the people served in any ongoing community life. Therefore the educational task is primarily technical—providing the team that is carrying out the service with the necessary continuing skills, knowledge, and understanding needed to do the job. To be sure, the life of the servicing team will need to be continually nurtured by Christ's love and a growing understanding of its meaning in terms of solidarity with each other and with those whom they serve. But its distinctive continuing educational task will be technical in nature.

In a *cathedral center* in a large city, the task might be to provide counseling, services of worship, a physical plant available for a variety of uses, coordination of a wider group of activities in other witnessing communities. The direct educational task would be that of providing continual training, both within the structure and through outside educational programs, for the skills of counseling, worship leadership, building maintenance, administration, etc. The indirect educational task would be the learning provided to those who participated in the services rendered in such things as beauty of architecture and liturgical form, or heightened self-understanding through counseling.

In a *monastic community,* such as Taizé in France, the

main task is that of serving Christ and the world within the discipline of the order. Therefore, the direct educational task would involve the years spent learning the disciplines of the monastic life as part of the community through study, practice, and commitment. At the same time it involves special skills needed for the services rendered within the community in worship, maintenance, etc., and outside in the world as workers and professionals. Part of its indirect educational task would be to provide a parable of the meaning of commitment by which others could learn to test their own forms of commitment to Christ.

In a retreat *center for dialogue* between the church and the world, such as Packard Manse in Stoughton, Massachusetts, or the Evangelical Academies in Europe, the direct educational task would be that of continued training of the academy staff. A center provides the resources for conferences and retreats related to the particular interest of the center, such as ecumenical dialogue, Jewish-Christian dialogue, dialogue between the church and the worker, the businessman, the civil servant, the politician, etc. Training is also needed in how to work with various types of groups, promote dialogue, and organize meetings. The service that such a community renders is educational through the forms of encounter that the center develops. These might take place on location or outside the center in such conferences as those planned for ski weekends, holiday outings, continuation groups among workers or executives; and they would aim at promoting greater understanding of the meaning of the gospel in the life of the world.

The distinctive characteristic of a task force structure is that it is gathered for a longer or a shorter duration to concentrate on a particular task that needs to be done. Therefore, its educational task is primarily that of a continuing dialogue that will enable it to have "eyes of faith" to see what Christ is doing in the world and to join him in his work. In this dialogue between the events of salvation and the events and needs of the world around them, the members of the task force will need help from various types of specialists. Thus they need not only one or more persons with theological training but also one or more persons who can provide resources for understanding the problem in which they are engaged. This enables the group to carry on a continual dialogue concerning the understanding of their task in the light of God's mission.

In a suburban force on *discrimination in housing,* the educational task would be that of seeking out the necessary data on the situation of discrimination in the real estate practices in the community and ways that might be available to cope with these. They would also need to learn what other groups are working in this field with whom they can cooperate and what key people are concerned with the issue either positively or as the main power blocks to change. At the same time, continual self-examination on attitudes of prejudice and the meaning of the gospel as it relates to their actions would be of great importance. Their indirect education of others would be largely an attempt to arouse the conscience of the local community.

In a task force ministering to *urban centers of power,* such as Metropolitan Associates of Philadelphia, the educational task would be shaped by the need to know and understand the political, educational, and social structures of the city, and to try to understand in what way the group can be a pressure group for change within the city structures. Technical knowledge of city planning, social science, etc., is of great importance to the functioning of the groups, as is continued study of the meaning of God's plan of salvation as it is viewed in the light of the needs of the city. The indirect educational task would be to act as a leaven in and through city life to help others gain new perspective on its needs and possible alternatives for improvement.

In a task force for *promoting community life* in a city housing project, the educational task would center on getting to know the community in which the members live and gaining insight into the prejudice, misunderstanding, and tensions that tend to block community life. At the same time, it would be important for the members to gain new self-understanding and insight into the way to bring people into relationship with one another through discussion in the way Christ breaks down barriers in their own lives, using concrete examples from their own good and bad experiences in promoting tenant participation. The indirect educational task would be that of helping others to learn new positive attitudes of concern for the possibility of life as an interdependent community. Such a task force might develop into a family-type structure as its concern for the larger community expanded, or it might find that it could disband altogether when its job was taken over by other community groups that formed to promote cooperation, such as a tenants' association, a community center, or building committees.

The distinctions between types of structures are for the sake of analysis and discussion and not because any one concrete instance exactly fits the typology. To make this clear, it is important to suggest educational tasks that might be found in the context of structures which include more than one type by the nature of their work.

A task force developing a ministry in a *situation of racial conflict,* such as the Delta Ministry of the National Council of Churches in Mississippi, might also take on the character of a structure of permanent availability as it began to develop needed services in a Negro community. Its educational task would be one of mutual education in which the people of the community educated the staff concerning the meaning of their existence and its problems, while staff in turn provided educational services in terms of self-help, community organization, how to deal with political structures, etc.

An *urban training center*, such as Metropolitan Urban Service Training in New York City, has a task of training that involves the development of action task forces in the metropolitan area where people can be trained in terms of reflection on their own involvement. At the same time, it offers certain types of training as a structure of permanent availability, such as intern programs, in-service training programs for ministers, leadership training for community leaders. The staff of such a center needs special training in skills similar to that of an evangelical academy, and the total educational task will involve as many different educational needs as are represented by the projects undertaken by the organization.

An *umbrella or zonal organization*, such as the National Council of Churches (or a similar regional council of churches), again has a variety of educational tasks according to its component parts. It might conceive of itself overall as an institution of permanent availability providing various services of coordination and representation for the denominations or churches in a particular zone or region. At the same time a national organization would be a task force seeking to address itself to international problems such as peace, racial revolution, urban development on a nationwide basis by means of the development of a variety of programs. A regional or zonal organization should be a task force addressing itself to problems particularly important in that region or zone. The educational task suited to each part of its structure would require great flexibility so that the various community structures would be helped to find their own pattern of nurture.

The concrete educational programs that emerge out of the various structures need to be determined, first of all, by participation of the serving community in the dialogue between God and his world; secondly, by the particular shape of the witnessing community and its function or task; and thirdly, by participation in the dialogue between the serving community and those who are served.[16]

PART THREE

The Structure of Christian Education—
Dialogue

Luke 24:13–35

"That very day two of them were going to a village named Emmaus, about seven miles from Jerusalem, and talking with each other about all these things that had happened. While they were talking and discussing together, Jesus himself drew near and went with them. But their eyes were kept from recognizing him. And he said to them, 'What is this conversation which you are holding with each other as you walk?' And they stood still, looking sad. Then one of them, named Cleopas, answered him, 'Are you the only visitor to Jerusalem who does not know the things that have happened there in these days?' And he said to them, 'What things?' And they said to him, 'Concerning Jesus of Nazareth, who was a prophet mighty in deed and word before God and all the people, and how our chief priests and rulers delivered him up to be condemned to death, and crucified him. But we had hoped that he was the one to redeem Israel.' . . . And he said to them, 'O foolish men, and slow of heart to believe all that the prophets have spoken! Was it not necessary that the Christ should suffer these things and enter into his glory?' And beginning with Moses and all the prophets, he interpreted to them in all the scriptures the things concerning himself.

"So they drew near to the village to which they were going. . . . When he was at table with them, he took the bread and blessed, and broke it, and gave it to them. And their eyes were opened and they recognized him; and he vanished out of their sight. They said to each other, 'Did not our hearts burn within us while he talked to us on the road, while he opened to us the scriptures?' And they rose that same hour and returned to Jerusalem. . . . Then they told what had happened on the road, and how he was known to them in the breaking of the bread."

The Gospel of Luke presents the story of Jesus as part of salvation history so that it may be clearly understood in relation to the past and the present history of the Jews, the church, and the Roman world.[1] This salvation history is presented by Luke as a movement along a way or path in which God works out his purpose in the world.[2] In Luke, ch. 24, we have a collection of resurrection traditions placed together in one continuous story of the resurrection. Here the disciples have followed their Lord from Galilee to Jerusalem and are about to follow him to the ends of the earth (Luke 23:5; Acts 1:8). Jesus' resurrection is the connecting link between his ministry and the church, for it reveals that Jesus is Lord of the world and that the disciples are called to witness to his Lordship by following his Way into the world.[3]

Luke 24:13–35 describes a dialogue along a road. Such dialogue is the structure or shape of Christian education for men, women, and children of all ages who continually have their "eyes opened" to see the Lord and his actions in the world when they are drawn into a living dialogue of study, worship, and action as the events of the Bible interact with the events of daily life. What happens each day illuminates their understanding of the way of the Lord in the Bible, and the happenings or events in the Bible illuminate their way following the Lord in the world. With "eyes of faith" they both know the Lord at work and witness with joy to the good news of God's love.

6

DIALOGUE WITH EYES OF FAITH

1. *A dialogical understanding of what God is doing in the world*

IF THE CHRISTIAN is called to join in God's mission of restoring men to their true created humanity by reconciling them to himself and one another, he needs to be helped to know concretely what this means.[1] In Chapter 3 we saw that God's plan and mission for the world is that he "desires all men to be saved and to come to the knowledge of the truth" (I Tim. 2:4). To be saved is to be given the power and the possibility of living in God's world as one who is truly human.[2] This humanity consists of a wholeness and health of relationship with God, neighbor, and self that can be seen both in Adam and in the life, death, and resurrection of the Second Adam. Man finds out his true humanity, who he truly is, through the example of obedient and loving Sonship revealed to us in Jesus Christ (Rom. 8:14–17; 14:6–7).

When we look to see what God is doing, the Bible gives us clues of what wholeness and health in creation look like: Isa. 25:6–9 tells us that God's purpose includes the gathering of his people together in a great feast where "he will swallow up death for ever, and . . . will wipe away tears from all faces"; Luke 4:18–19 (Isa. 61:1–2) tells us that Jesus views his ministry in conjunction with God's plan of deliverance for all men when the good news is preached to the poor, captives released, and the blind given sight (Ps. 146). The same sort of description occurs in Matt. 11:2–6 when Jesus points to his miracles of healing and to proclamation of the good news of God's love for all men as signs that he is the Messiah, the one sent from God to establish the New Age of God's deliverance. Today as we live in this New Age of the Messiah, we know God's mission to be that of completing his act of redemption of the world in Jesus Christ by bringing liberty, release, and full humanity to all men. In this sense we know what God is doing because he has told us of his plan and promise through the words and actions of his Son.

But the problems still remain. How does this knowledge of God's mission become concrete in terms of the Christian's understanding of where and how he should join in God's mission of making men truly human? This knowledge is given to us through the Holy Spirit as we participate in the *dialogue of Christian education—the dialogue between God and his world that is heard by the witnessing community as an invitation of Christ to join in his mission in the world*. Response to this dialogue involves a lot of risk because we may not understand God's mission or the world situation well enough to make the right choice in our actions. There is risk because we are often hurt by the world when we dare to love it and become involved in its struggles for freedom and justice. But the Christian is not left alone in the decision or action, for the context of his response is the witnessing community that shares the risk and the joy of joining in God's mission through concrete actions. And his decision is made out of a continual dialogue with Christ, who continues to guide and nurture him through his Spirit.

A parable of the way in which Christ leads men to decision and commitment in dialogue may be seen in Luke 24:13–35. The first thing that is clear is that here dialogue takes place *on the road* to Emmaus (v. 13). This means that it takes place in the world where Christ is at work and where he leads his disciples to the ends of the earth (Acts 1:8). Jesus is present with them along the road in their daily occupations as he helps them to see the meaning of God's promise interpreted in the Scriptures (Luke 24:27). The second thing we see in the story is that the dialogue happens as they are *"talking and discussing together."* Dialogue takes place in human community. This is where Christ nurtures us and informs us through participation in the words and actions of others.

The third thing we see is that the dialogue reached its climax in a self-revealing *event.* As Christ makes himself known to the disciples, the breaking of bread becomes the event of faith, the moment when the disciples gain the "eyes of faith" to see the reality of their living Lord and the events of the past days, including the talk on the road, suddenly fall into place (vs. 30–32). "A-ha! Now we see what it was all about. Why he died. That he is alive!" Thus dialogue involves an event of faith, a commitment of faith by which men take with ultimate seriousness the fact that Christ makes himself known to them in and through the "stuff" of this world, and believe that this is what makes sense of the world as the object of God's love and redemption. This is the moment of intuition made possible by the structure of the dialogue in which Christ helps men to see the relations of God's action to the world.

The fourth thing we see is that the dialogue issues in an *act of witness.* The disciples run to tell the others "what had happened on the road, and how he was known to them in the breaking of the bread" (v. 35). In their action of faith they make it possible for others to gain the "eyes of faith" in seeing the way God speaks in word and action to his world. Dialogue involves us in the risk of an action of witness. It leads us to make the commitment to join Christ at a concrete point in history and to point to his presence by our words and actions. In this process of dialogue,

Christ enables God's word to guide us and sustain us so that we can make our commitment to join God's mission of establishing the New Age where the blind see, the lame walk, and liberty from every human bondage is proclaimed.

2. *The structure of Christian education understood as dialogue*

The structure of Christian education may be understood as dialogue in two senses. One is that Christian education is primarily concerned with the dialogue between God and his world. The other is that Christian education involves both teacher and pupil in a conversation concerning the meaning of the way God speaks to his world. The dialogue between God and his world in which God speaks through word and event in history, revealing his plan and purpose for mankind, is the *dialogue of Christian education* (Heb. 1:1-2). This dialogue is *made alive* to the hearers through the Spirit of Christ, which is at work in and through men's lives. It is *heard* by the witnessing community who understand God's words and actions in the light of the Biblical message of God's love for the world. They remember what God has done, and they point to his actions in the present, celebrating his actions and confessing his name. It is *learned* by those who participate with the witnessing community in hearing and responding to God's word and action. The structure of Christian education is dialogical because it is concerned with the way that God speaks to men and with the way that men participate together in responding to God's word in the locus of the witnessing community.[3]

The dialogue that involves both teacher and pupil in conversation in Christian education finds its counterpart in secular education. For man's God-given talent of language is employed in a continual dialogue of listening, questioning, and responding to God and other men (Gen. 2:19). *Dialogue* in the general sense of the word is "a conversation between two or more persons."[4] In such conversation men are able to express themselves in relation to other men and to the world in which they live. Because all education takes place in the context of such human relationships, its structure should always be dialogical. As we saw in Chapter 2, the process of education is one of actualizing and modifying the development of the total person in and through dialogical relationships. And Christian education is distinguished from other forms of education simply by its perspective which sees Christ and the Holy Spirit as the teachers, and human teachers as participants in Christ's invitation to join in God's mission.

The word "structure" refers to the "interrelation of parts as dominated by the general character of the whole."[5] We have already seen that structure as a sociological term does not indicate a fixed pattern because human groupings are in a constant state of change or process. Rather, it is simply a description of a particular moment in process so that a social unit may be studied. The word "structure" as it refers to education retains this fluid character in that human knowledge and understanding are in a constant state of change. But it places its emphasis on the way the particular parts of an educational discipline are interrelated, and because these parts are not human, the pattern of interrelationship remains fairly stable. Thus in his book *The Process of Education,* Jerome Bruner is able to say that to learn the structure of a discipline is to learn "how things are related."[6]

Bruner emphasizes learning the structure of a particular educational discipline rather than its content, for two reasons.[7] The first is that it enables a student to think intuitively so that he can view a problem in terms of his grasp of the total structure of the discipline which will give him insight into possible solutions. The second is that the structure or interrelation of a discipline such as mathematics or history remains the same regardless of how simple or difficult the problem. Thus children can be taught this structure at an early age and helped to think intuitively and creatively as they increase in their ability to confront more difficult and complicated problems. This makes the curriculum of a subject or a discipline a "spiral curriculum" which gets more and more difficult as the student progresses, but goes round and round through the same structure of the discipline at each level.[8]

The structure of the discipline of history is a dialogue that teacher and student carry on between the events (and the systems of human relationships involved in events) of the past and of the present. Biblical history, which forms the basis of our knowledge of the saving acts of God in the events of history, has this same dialogical structure. Here, however, the dialogue in which the teacher and the student participate concerns the events of the past and of the present that are understood in the light of God's revelation of his plan and purpose for the world. In teaching Biblical history according to the suggestions of Bruner, those who participate as teachers would be concerned to help the student think intuitively about the meaning of God's actions in relation to the problems of their own lives. Such teaching could begin at a very early age as it sought in a common dialogue of teacher and student to help the child understand the way God makes himself known in the history of salvation, and the pattern of his self-revelation as a God who is faithful to his promise as he works out the redemption of the world through his love.

In a spiral curriculum the child or adult could be continually helped to understand the basic pattern of the way God relates himself to man and the world as illustrated in more and more difficult or problematic content. For instance, a four-year-old could learn that God cares about the problems of his people and works to set them free from bondage in a simple story of Moses and the exodus, or of the way Jesus helped and healed men; and fifty years later the same person would still be exploring the relationship of God's saving acts to the problems of evil not only in the exodus and in Easter, but also in Job and in Revelation. Thus the student and the teacher would both grow in their understanding of the structure of the way God acts in history and in their ability to intuit the meaning of God's action in new and unexplored events in their own world. In such a process of continual dialogue between the teacher and the student concerning the events of salvation history, the student would find that the basic structure of Biblical history is always the same: a dialogue of word and action between God and his world by which God reveals himself as one who loves and cares for his children.

3. *Bible study as a major locus of dialogue in a witnessing community*

Biblical history is not all of Christian education, which includes everything that happens in the total context of the witnessing community in the world by which Christ extends his invitation to join in God's mission. Yet Biblical history is the foundation of our knowledge of the way God in Christ is at work. The Bible is the record of God's self-revelation and is therefore a gift of grace that enables us to enter into the dialogue between God and his world. It not only helps us to gain the "eyes of faith" to see God's action in the world but it also equips us to join in that action. In and through study the Holy Spirit teaches us to respond to God's love by acknowledging God as our Father sharing his love with our brothers (Gal. 4:4–7).[9]

There is no one way to study the Bible, but the understanding we have gained concerning the dialogical structure of the discipline of Biblical history and the dialogical structure of Christian education in which Christ equips men to join in God's mission are a strong indication that Bible study takes place in the framework of a dialogue—

dialogue between God and man and between man and man in which Christ grants to men the intuition of faith to understand the events of God's world. In this dialogue men do the talking, studying, thinking, praying, but Christ is always present whether he is recognized or not (Luke 24:13–35; Matt. 18:20). Sometimes he is present but ignored, waiting to be recognized and known as the Christ. At other times he is recognized and allowed to enter into the conversation by the power of his Spirit.[10]

If we return to the dialogue of Luke, ch. 24, we may find clues by which to understand the dialogue of Bible study. Bible study should be a dialogue *on the road*. The word of God comes alive in the midst of men and women gathered together for Bible study if they are a witnessing community already on the road. The context of the study has to be men and women already seeking to follow Christ day by day in the world, who see this study as the very "bread of life" by which God sustains them in their journey. The community does not seek for a detailed road map of their journey, but they seek to know what the Bible is saying and what it meant to those who spoke and wrote the words so that they can understand the journey of faith in which they are already involved. Because the dialogue occurs in a community on the road, there is never any separation between word and act, between study and service. The community is "in service" and one of the ways Christ sustains it is through study of the Bible. Thus the kind of debate so familiar in books on Christian education written in the 1940's about whether you teach about life or about the Bible is irrelevant.[11] The witnessing community is gathered around its function, and the study is part of the equipment for its task of service. A task force community serving in the area of public education is just as much in need of Bible study in the dialogue of its Christian education as the community of permanent availability, which provides daily services of worship and emergency counseling and referral in a business district.

Bible study should also be *together*. Of course, individual study, preparation, and meditation are important to understanding the text, but the dialogical nature of study means that it reaches its most complete form when it takes place in a group. Alone we can always refuse to listen to all the aspects of the text. Alone we can easily grow weary of trying to go about the very difficult process of interpreting God's word. However, in a group we find mutual encouragement and mutual teaching. No matter who is the leader, each one teaches the other through his ideas and concerns. New ideas that never occurred in solitary suddenly emerge as a neighbor begins to speak of the meaning of a text from his point of view. People come to a better understanding of what God is saying through the text and also to a better understanding of one another. Thus as men and women open themselves to one another in the light of God's word, the Spirit helps to shape their relationships of mutual concern and love, self-discipline and forbearance. In group Bible study, people can learn to listen if they are too quick to talk, or to talk if they are too hesitant to have an opinion of their own.

The East Harlem Protestant Parish in New York City has found weekly group Bible study so important for the mutual growth in understanding of the Bible, of self, and of the problems of the community that the *Daily Bible Reading* lectionary used for study and preaching is designed completely as a tool for group study and not for private meditation.[12] The introductions to the passage to be studied for the week try to bring to bear a knowledge of the exegetical problems and of the situation of the people engaged in study in such a way that the introduction helps equip the leaders and participants to consider the critical issues raised by the text. Their group thinking in turn provides the basis for the Sunday sermon on the same text. No attempt is made to water the lectionary down to simple verses and poetic thoughts, which can be read for one minute before jumping into bed. In fact, it is hoped that the introduction will lead to further preparation by the reading of commentaries and thought concerning questions raised. This further preparation is made much more likely because the people know they will have a chance to make use of their preparation in group discussion. For many, the lectionary is not understandable apart from group discussion, but neither is the Bible, and there are not many laymen today who find the reading of the Bible without group study a very rewarding task.

The dialogue of Bible study also includes an *event* of faith. It is approached with real seriousness just because something real is happening here. In the study, a witnessing community becomes a part of its heritage. It finds out who its ancestors are and what the events were that shaped their lives. By an event of faith they enter into the events of salvation history so that they become their events, their faith, their history. Just as Christ was known in the event of the breaking of the bread and is still known as Christians gather to celebrate the event of his death and resurrection, he is known in the breaking open of the Word. This moment when the Word comes alive and becomes, not what is printed or spoken, but the living reality and commitment of the gathered community is a moment of intuition granted to followers of Christ by the power of the Holy Spirit. Just as the Hebrew people celebrated God's covenant by the recital of the mighty acts, these actions in the breaking open of the Word become eternally contemporaneous with us. In this manner the power of the Holy Spirit enables men and women to know the events of salvation as their own so that they may live by their promise day by day in the world.[13]

Such events of faith occur in many and various ways. Often they are not dramatic and are hardly noticed, but they are nevertheless real. Clearly such happenings occur not just in one study, but over a long period of time where a group stays with its study through thick and thin, through

boredom, poor attendance, dominating ministers, and all
the rest. For the Bible does not come alive in our lives
unless we allow it to be a continual part of our daily thinking and conversation.[14] Yet over the years the spiral curriculum of God's mighty acts molds and shapes the lives
of members of a witnessing community so that all of life
is informed by the little surprises of insight and joy as
people suddenly recognize themselves in a passage or see
the words of a passage come alive in their midst. A man
at a party will suddenly find himself arguing about the
interpretation of the passage from last week or advising the
preacher about what to say on Sunday. A woman will
hear in Bible study discussion the very thing she refused
to hear when someone had tried to warn her of a mistake
in handling a problem of human relations the day before. A
man who walks a picket line for the first time will suddenly discover what it means to say, "Let my people go."
A child who takes the blame for his friend's misdeed in
school may "hear" the words, "Bear one another's burdens." A task force will see the healing ministry of Christ
take on new meaning as its efforts help convince the government to construct a community hospital. And a community will find in real events that, in fact, the lame do
learn to walk and the blind to see as the events of God's
salvation become their own events.

The dialogue of Bible study should include *actions of
witness* as well, for if the events come alive in the hearts
and minds of people, they also will take shape in their
actions. The desire to run to share the gospel with others
is not limited to the disciples in Emmaus or to pentecostal
preachers. It is a desire that everyone has who knows the
joy of God's love. A desire to "gossip the gospel," to tell
the good news about what is happening to everyone who
will listen. In the world in which we live, talk is cheap,
and it is important that a witnessing community be able
to witness by the life it leads of mutual support of one

another and of service to others. This is how it allows the word to be known that in Christ men are made free and whole. By concrete actions of witness, the community spells out the Word of God so that those who are blind are helped to know how to see, those who are in prison are told of liberation, those who are sad are comforted. The concrete word addressed to the concrete need of the world becomes the witness of those who have heard that liberating word in their own lives in such a way that they are free to share it with others.

Dialogue is the structure of Christian education because it is in and through dialogue that Christ nurtures us to join in God's mission in the world. The dialogue goes on continually between God and his world, and the witnessing community is called to participate in the dialogue so that their lives may be shaped by it and their eyes may be opened to see what God is doing in the world and to join in his action. The dialogue itself is in constant change and movement, but the structure, the way God speaks to us in and through his living word, remains the same. The dialogue is between God and his world, and he allows us to listen so that we may join in. However, when the church tries to capture the dialogue of Christian education and make it a conversation that goes round and round as the same old story among the same few people, then it will become a dialogue like the one in the first part of the story on the road to Emmaus, a dialogue in which they talked and talked but did not even know that Jesus was there.

DIALOGUE IN NATURAL
SOCIAL GROUPINGS

1. Natural social groupings as a context for dialogue

IF THE DIALOGUE of Christian education goes on continually between God and his world, and the witnessing community is called to participate in this dialogue, it must be willing to let the points of dialogue be indicated by the social structures of the world. It is the witnessing community *in the world* that is the context of the dialogue and it is the witnessing community that needs to form all of its life around that world as it follows the mission of its Lord. This is to say that the disciplines of theology and sociology must be in constant dialogue with one another as the church considers how it may participate in Christ's invitation to join in God's mission in the world.[1] Its "missionary structures" (structures that are fashioned for participation in God's mission) take their shape from the social groupings of the world. This has already been seen in Part II, where the types of structures suggested were those most relevant to the type of world in which we live. Here the same principle needs to be applied to specific contexts where the educational dialogue may take place in any type of witnessing community.

An important location for educational dialogue is in social groupings where people naturally communicate with one another. A factory worker talks more readily to another worker than to a minister or to the boss. A teen-ager talks more readily to a friend in his group than to a teacher or a parent. A skiing enthusiast likes to talk to other skiing enthusiasts whether they are talking about war, sex, politics, or skiing. Thus, although the nature of God's activity in Christ is that it cuts across all natural lines and barriers and unites men and women in the common bond of Christ's love, the witnessing community in joining that activity does not require men to come into new and artificial structures before it will take any interest in them. After all, they may not *know* that they are united in Christ and they may *never hear* that they are, if the witnessing community does not point to God's mission in terms that the world can hear. So, besides concern for bringing men together across lines and helping them to gain new insights into their common predicaments and their common solidarity, the witnessing community is concerned to involve itself in dialogue within the natural social groups that it finds in any given place or time.

In Chapter 4 we saw that although in modern society the mobile small family unit is still a "dominant locus of valuing behavior," it is no longer the relevant structure in terms of community life and the public realm. Other structures such as the "production team" and the "peer group" also provide the day-to-day social interchange by which the lives of people are shaped and molded.[2] The "production team" finds its meaningful relationships in the job to be done which serves as a center of all forms of social intercourse. The "peer group," on the other hand, finds its meaningful relationships in the common age and interest of its members. A peer group is a group of "people like (equal to) me." Just as the "production team" has taken over from the family as the dominant grouping in terms of working relationships, the peer group has tended to take over from the family as the dominant grouping in terms of leisure relationships. Thus the family as the main unit of social living has ceased to be a reality in the middle class even as it was never true in the working class.[3]

Although the peer group is usually identified with teen-age culture, it is used here to refer to a general human phenomenon of all ages. In modern American society not only teen-agers, but all ages form peer groups in which all those in the same group tend to think and act in the same way. Not only teen-agers and delinquents but also suburbanites and business executives tend to dress, act, and think alike as they strive for acceptance among their peers.[4] Even the lonely individual in our society frequently longs for a group that can give him support and direction. And this kind of individual can often be helped by providing a social context where he feels himself to be part of a group. To be sure, there are some people who are still lonely even though they follow the crowd, and there are others who enjoy being "rugged individualists" and want to stay that way. Yet my experience is that most men today search for meaning in social relationships that extend beyond their own lives as individuals and families.

2. Peer groups as a negative and a positive factor in educational dialogue

People in the churches have long been aware of the negative aspects of peer groups. They have tried to turn "back the clock," to cling to family structures in order to save outworn denominational structures, and have found "families" looking to them to save the sinking ship. The result is that proponents of the good old days in family and church have enjoyed all the scathing sociological analyses of what is wrong with American culture, hardly recognizing that insofar as they refuse to change with the times, they are in fact enjoying their own swan song.

Peer group behavior does make it clear that men *no longer think independently* (if they ever did). Men think alike; that is, they think according to the way the group and the culture of which they are a part conditions them to think.[5] If "pacifism," "death of God," "new math," "the Beatles," are *avant-garde,* then they belong to the thinking of a whole group. The group tends to develop its own O.K. language by which to express common thoughts and to listen to its own teachers who speak their language.

Men not only think alike in peer groups, they also *act alike.* They are that same old bunch of sheep that Isaiah talks about (ch. 53:6). Not only children and youth, but adults as well, dress like their friends. Wearing heavy rubber raincoats in hot summer weather, sneakers in a blizzard, one earring, a beard and no overcoat, dresses that look like tents, suits of gray flannel is normal behavior if it happens to be the style of the group. People have very similar sex patterns, eating patterns, TV tastes, and all the rest. Men in peer groups like to *go places together* and often prefer to go places only when they are sure a lot of people just like themselves will be present. They go to things simply because "everyone will be there."

But what if we look at peer-group behavior to see it as a positive factor in educational dialogue? The first thing we notice is that these supposedly strange group patterns are not so new or strange. In fact, men are social beings, created to live in relationship, and to find their own identity in relationship to other men and to God. Therefore, men always tend to think and act like others and to want to be together in community. The only difference in our own time is that the group providing the value system is not the family, except insofar as it too is part of the larger TV culture, and it is certainly not the church with its Protestant business ethic. To see this, all we have to do is look at any church youth group. The group does not want to do what the parents want. And the group will not function at all, whether to worship or dance, unless the aims and goals have a relationship to the existing peer-group style of life. The only way a youth group can combine youth from different cliques or small peer groups is by bringing together the different groups. Individuals will not come if their "friends are not there." The same thing tends to be true for theologians, truck drivers, and bank presidents. The only way to be sure that they will consider a meeting worthy of their attendance is if they are sure a certain number of their "peers" will be present.

Members of a peer group *think alike,* and this has distinct advantages for educational dialogue. The significant factor is not that youth will not listen to adults and bank presidents to truck drivers, but that they *will* listen to each other. Educational dialogue in the setting of their own group will go on as the members teach each other in their own terms and according to their familiar patterns of thought. From the Christian point of view, all teachers are participating teachers as they participate together with Christ in extending the invitation to join God's mission and participate together with others in mutual edification.[6] What better way for the group to engage in dialogue than by means of its own teachers and its own language?[7]

Peer groups *act alike,* and this too has distinct educational advantages. Christian education involves the total person in a total community as Christ shapes and nurtures the lives of men, women, and children. This means that people's lives are shaped as they participate in a community, as they participate in life together and with Christ. Out of this participation they develop a style of life that helps to keep them open to Christ's direction yet equips them to be able to serve in the world.[8] The advantage of the peer group is that it provides an opportunity to affect changes in behavior through the group style. While recognizing that a witnessing community is at best a leaven in society, it is nevertheless possible to consider how it can minister to a peer group in such a way as to help it alter its style in the direction of greater wholeness and health for the members of the group. In a group of young people, if it were the style to study and work hard to get ahead in school, many wonderful things could happen to the children's school records. If it were the style to save money rather than to spend it on show items and food, habits of responsible use of money would be improved. If it were the style *not* to get pregnant at an early age, many unfortunate marriages might not take place.[9]

Peer groups go places and do things *together*. This is clearly a disadvantage if we prefer people to be asocial. It is a disadvantage if we resent the fact that if they do not go to church together (as in urban centers), they do not go at all, or if they do all go to church together (as in suburbia), they turn the church into a rather inferior social club. However, it becomes an advantage as soon as we begin to think about people in groups and expect them to be in groups. Then size and type of group become simply matters of function. People like to be in large groups of a hundred or more for celebrations, rallies, demonstrations, and the like. They feel more joyful, or more militant, when they see all the other people, because in a mass society a group is hardly "seen" until it numbers in the hundreds and thousands. The part of educational dialogue that involves this type of public gathering should be geared to bringing together large groups so that they can express their solidarity in this manner.

Many adults in our complex society feel the weight of depersonalization and need the support of a small group to help provide identity and assurance. Here Bible study groups and small task force groups can help to meet the need to be together in small numbers to carry on dialogue. Yet children and youth tend to enjoy being with a larger group of peers. They like to be packed together and to go with the crowd and it is in this crowd or peer group that the educational dialogue goes forward in its most natural setting. The point here is simply that as the dialogue goes on between God and the world, it is the job of the witnessing community to search out what God is doing, to seek positive ways of working in the world of which it is a part.

3. *The peer group as a natural grouping among children and youth*

Peer group behavior exists throughout our society and affects the lives of all of us. However, it is most prominently visible in the lives of children and youth, and it is therefore helpful to look at this setting as an example of how the peer group can promote learning through dialogue.[10] In a particular peer group program of education for children or youth, large groups of at least fifty to a hundred children are important so that the children can feel that they are together. The children like to be together. In fact, they like to be crowded. Given some skill in leadership and group dynamics, the problems of discipline tend to decrease rather than increase when a large number of children are together. A pattern can be set for the group by a consistent routine and schedule and the following of certain basic rules of safety and behavior that will be enforced by the majority of the group itself. Group pressure will tend to bring children "into line" who in a group of three to ten are almost impossible to handle. Somehow, children do not feel the need to "act out" nearly as much in large groups as in small ones. And group pressure to conformity sets the style of behavior and participation that is helpful to the educational dialogue.[11]

In such a peer group the main teaching dialogue takes place among the members of the group itself. The director of the program is an enabler who helps the children and other teaching participants to teach themselves. Thus one trained and experienced leader can serve as director of such a program for a hundred children with the help of one other strong troubleshooter and ten other participating teachers who need not be adults or specifically trained.[12]

The children learn from their peers as they share together in their learning through drama, music, quiz shows, crafts projects, questions and answers, parties, etc.[13] Even their noise and the comments they make in such a group program contribute to the dialogue when the comments reflect involvement in what is happening in a play or a quiz show.

Thus if such a group were to study the book of The Acts, they would so participate in the study that it would be their own study and a study into which they were drawn by a dialogue of the events of the early church and their own lives. Through informal plays in which the children made up their own lines they would experience Paul's shipwrecks and Peter's agony in the segregation issue. At the same time as the actors would be having a wonderful time "showing off," the rest of the group would be learning some basic facts while having a wonderful experience seeing their friends make fools of themselves and "sounding on them" just as they would in any informal setting. A panel or a quiz show might serve to bring out for all the children the inner resentments and fears that are caused by segregation in our own society as "Paul and Silas bound in jail" are compared to the freedom fighters whom they know in their own church and community, and Peter's refusal to eat with Gentiles is compared to segregated churches of today. A bright-orange enamel pin in the form of a flame might identify them all around the community and at school as those who have been sent into difficult and dangerous tasks following the Lord by the power of the Holy Spirit. Together they enjoy the dialogue between God and his world and enter into that dialogue with a spontaneity born of being in their own natural social groupings. If you asked them why they came, a few would say because they liked it, but most would simply reply, "Because my friends all go there," for the peer group is their center of life.

4. Dialogue in other social groups

The discussion concerning peer groups is not intended to say that they are the only point of dialogical education or that the dialogue between God and his world is heard only in groups, for God speaks in many and various ways. Rather, peer groups are an example of how educational structures of mission have to take place in and through natural social groupings. Certainly the *production team* is equally important in society and needs to be carefully studied by witnessing communities who seek to minister to the needs of men in the working and public sphere of life. Just as the peer group educational method with children described here grew out of the experience of a witnessing community in its ministry to large groups of urban youth, the experience of other witnessing communities will reveal other forms of educational dialogue with production teams as they seek to minister in this sphere. Whatever shape the particular method takes, it should allow the freedom of dialogue and the freedom to follow the function of the particular group.

We have already seen a different type of dialogue in the discussion of *small-group Bible study*. This same type of small group is also valuable for older youth when they reach the stage of wanting a chance to question everything and to express their own ideas. In addition, *other types of small groupings* and work with individuals are a valuable part of educational dialogue when they are in natural settings. A teacher and students learn more by taking a trip to the beach or baking cookies at home in groups of two to five than they do sitting down around a table with books, if the teacher really cares enough about the students to be a participant with them in the experience.[14] Small groups designed as task forces to work out or study a problem or to render a service to others are wonderful centers of dialogue where the students can work together in learning and serving. Whether visiting the home, playing, studying, or working together, the teacher plays the role of an enabler who lets the group learn through its own dialogue and thus by his care and concern for the members of the group. Whatever the social grouping, the educational dialogue should be allowed to follow the lines of the interrelationships in the group as with "eyes of faith" members of a witnessing community seek to see the good gifts that God has given in the structures of his world and use them in such a way as to enable the dialogue between God and his world to be heard.

PART FOUR

The Method of Christian Education—
Participation

I Corinthians 10:16–17; 11:23–26

"The cup of blessing which we bless, is it not a participation in the blood of Christ? The bread which we break, is it not a participation in the body of Christ? Because there is one bread, we who are many are one body, for we all partake of the one bread. . . .

"For I received from the Lord what I also delivered to you, that the Lord Jesus on the night when he was betrayed took bread, and when he had given thanks, he broke it, and said, 'This is my body which is for you. Do this in remembrance of me.' In the same way also the cup, after supper, saying, 'This cup is the new covenant in my blood. Do this, as often as you drink it, in remembrance of me.' For as often as you eat this bread and drink the cup, you proclaim the Lord's death until he comes."

These words of Paul concerning the Lord's Supper come to us in the context of discussions of practical problems in the congregation at Corinth. Chapter 10:16–17 is a description of the feast of the Lord's Supper as part of a discussion begun in ch. 8 concerning the freedom to eat food offered to idols and the problems of participating in heathen feasts. Chapter 11:23–26 gives our earliest account of the Lord's Supper and a description of the way the first-century church celebrated Holy Communion in the context of a discussion of the problems of gluttony and drunkenness at the common meal. The two key words in the passages are "body of Christ" and "participation." The words "body of Christ" are used frequently by Paul and usually refer to Christ and not to the church. The body of Christ is the risen and glorified body of Christ with which believers are united by the power of God's Spirit and with which they will be fully united at his second coming.[1] It is also the community of Christ's people, or the church. The members of the church are members of Christ's body and are the instruments of his work in the world (I Cor. 12:12, 27). The word "participation" (communion, fellowship) is a translation of the word *koinōnia*, which means having a share in something or fellowship together in the action.[2] Christians have a share in Christ's body because in the eating and drinking they also express their fellowship and unity together in the body of Christ as it is represented in the community of the church.

This word, participation, provides a method of Christian education in the same twofold sense of the above definition. As participation is to have a share in something, to be an actual part of it, an indispensable method of Christian education is that the child or adult be an actual part of the life of Christ as it is lived out in the witness and service of the congregation. Thus the Christian learns by actually being a part of and having a share in the work that the congregation performs as the hands and feet of Christ in the world. As participation is to have fellowship together in the action, so the method of Christian education includes the relationships that are formed by being together with others and sharing their style of life in the witnessing community (Phil. 1:5).

TEACHER AND STUDENT PARTICIPATION

1. Participation as a method of Christian education

CHRISTIAN EDUCATION is the means by which the church can participate in Christ's invitation to all people to join in God's mission. We have seen that the context in which Christ extends this invitation is the witnessing community in the world, and that the structure of Christ's work of nurture is the dialogue between God and man and man and man. The method of procedure by which this dialogue goes on in the witnessing community is that of participation— participation in Christ and in the life of his community, and participation with one another in witness, study, and service. We participate or "have a share in" Christ not only through the Sacraments, where he unites us to his heavenly body by the power of his Holy Spirit, but also in the work of Christ as he grants us the power of forgiveness and new life to join him in his work of reconciliation in the world (Phil. 3:20–21; I Cor. 10:16; Acts 1:8). We participate or "have fellowship together in the action" of the witnessing community not only as Christ unites us to one another by the power of his Spirit through the Sacraments, but also as he unites us in service to our brothers as one community with one Lord and one job to do (Eph. 4:4–6; John 17:20–21; Matt. 25:31–40).

The word "participation" (koinonia, fellowship, community) is not only a key word in the Biblical understanding of our life in Christ. It has long been a familiar word in the field of education. In the beginning of the twentieth century, George Albert Coe made this word, already popular in the progressive movements of his time, a key word in his writings on education.[1] Coe and Harrison S. Elliott developed the method of group discussion because they saw the aim of democracy as that of securing the active participation of every individual and they wanted to stress the ideas of equality, horizontal learning experience, and liberation of the human intelligence to think creatively.[2] And long before Coe and Elliott, the church of the fourth century was training its catechumens in a three-year course of learning by doing, and the church of John Calvin's time was viewing education as an endless process of participation in the school of Christ.[3]

Nor is the idea of participation limited to Christian perspectives on education. As was pointed out in Chapter 2, in educational discussions there is stress on teaching as part of a production team. This type of team makes it possible for the teachers to participate with one another and with the children in the teaching task and at the same time encourages the students to work in the same sort of teams while they learn by participation. Yet the popularity of this word has not seemed to have much effect on the normal structures of church life today. The structures remain by and large hierarchical. The minister or teacher tells others what to do, and little opportunity for genuine participation in decision making, education, or worship is possible. Only when the whole structure of the witnessing community becomes one of participation together with Christ in God's mission will it be possible for participation to be an authentic word in the method of Christian education.[4]

2. Participation through team teaching

We have already seen that the role of the teacher in Christian education is that of a participant.[5] There is only one kind of teacher regardless of the age group being taught—that is the *participating teacher*. The teacher is a participant because Christ is the teacher through the power of his Spirit at work in men's lives. Christian education is participation in Christ's invitation, and those who aid in this invitation are participating teachers. The teacher is also a participant because he never teaches alone. If the context of education is the witnessing community, it follows that *all* the members of that community do the teaching. Each one teaches the other through their life together, so that together the whole community is a teaching team. Lastly, the teacher is a participant because the teacher participates in the educational dialogue along with the students, simply enabling them to teach themselves by providing the necessary tools and insights as they join together in study and service.

In such a context the most natural form of teaching is that of *team teaching*. Team teaching allows each one on the "production team" to make a contribution to the work and at the same time serves to remind the teachers that their job is to work together with others for their joy (II Cor. 1:24). In this manner the teaching team, be it a whole Bible study group that rotates in its leadership responsibility, or a team of urban planning experts who help a task force in its work with city planning, or a team of youth and adults who work in a peer-group program for children, becomes a representative of the function of the whole witnessing community as it joins in Christ's work of equipping the saints for God's mission.

Team teaching is an important part of peer-group education with children.[6] It affords many opportunities to play to the strengths of the untrained teacher. It permits the untrained youth or parent to work with the children so that he can make use of his knowledge and experience of the children's culture in relating them naturally. In peer-group education, emphasis is always put on ways in which children with leadership ability can form the teaching core both informally through group participation, skits, etc., and formally when they are selected to work as assistant teachers in a particular program. Youth or young adults who are slightly older make good teachers for youth. These are the ones who set the patterns every day on the streets and who can communicate best with those whom they teach. This also gives the younger teachers valuable experience in their responsibility to serve others as a part of a family-type community. Lastly, peer-group teaching makes it possible for a teacher to be a valuable part of the program even if he cannot read a lesson plan or make speeches in front of large groups. The opportunities for developing natural leadership in such a program are great. The main hindrance is that teachers have been so brainwashed by what they have always been told that they feel they must have a small class and individual responsibility just because this is a prestige symbol associated with other church schools they have known.[7]

A crucial ingredient of all team teaching is *in-service training*. Not only are the students being trained "in service" with the teachers, but also the teachers are constantly learning through their experience on the teaching team. In-service training implies that team teaching takes place in the context of the total life of the witnessing community. Those who come forward to teach are already being nurtured and sustained in other parts of the community life. The Bible study leader finds that his task is not so difficult because he has already discussed and acted out the passage as part of a peer-group teaching team. Or the leader of a discussion on open enrollment in the schools finds that his previous experience on the executive committee of a parents association helps him to interpret the resistance of the principal to this particular idea. A teen-ager helping to lead a retreat for another youth group will find that he has already gained valuable tips in group dynamics by his participation as a teaching team with younger children. All of them find their job much easier because they are never alone. Others in the group are sharing leadership with them. Because team teaching takes place in the total context of the life of the community, the teacher finds that he is called to participate in extending the same invitation of Christ to others that he himself is constantly receiving.

In-service training also means that in many situations a teacher can begin to serve right away with no special training or skill. As part of a team, he can find the job best suited to his ability and knowledge, be it making up the attendance list, serving refreshments, cutting wood, preparing a service of worship or a statistical report. Because he serves in a group, the teacher is free to learn new skills and develop unsuspected talents as he enters into new areas of teaching and leadership. He learns more quickly if given help and encouragement because he has others who are doing it with him and does not have to sink or swim by himself. Often people who have never dared or cared to give time and energy to teaching others find new interest and energy as they become involved in creative ventures in team teaching.

Team teaching means *group planning*. This does not mean that one or more persons should not think out the overall program ahead of time. In fact, good group planning presupposes that at least one person has given the meeting prior thought and preparation and can come to the meeting with suggestions and outlines for discussion. Thus team teaching in Bible study might mean that a group of leaders would come together to study the text ahead of time as their preparation. But they in turn would need at least one person who had studied and planned for their meeting. Or a team meeting to prepare a peer-group program for youth would expect someone with more experience and training to give guidance in the overall themes and approaches, and to help the group select the best activities and forms of teaching for a particular lesson. However, team planning means that the various members are encouraged to take responsibility as they are able. In a peer-group program, one person would plan a play with a group of children, another might write a song, another might do research on the Bible passage for the following week, while another might take responsibility for setting up the room for the meeting. In planning a retreat, various people would take responsibility for the parts of the program and the living arrangements. An illustration of the types of outlines that can be used as a basis for creative expansion in group planning for children may be found in the *Christian Education Handbook*.[8]

Team teaching is not the only form of teaching. Yet it is uniquely suited to the mutual education of witnessing communities as Christ equips them for their task in the world. Whatever the form of teaching, it needs to be one that involves the participation of the teacher and student together and should be related directly to the particular function that the group is being educated to perform. Many of the above ideas concerning team teaching emerged in an inner-city setting where the people did not have obvious leadership abilities or extensive educational opportunities. They apply in many other situations, yet the most important thing is not whether they apply, but the way in which they emerged. Insights into "missionary structures" emerge when we are willing to take stock of the world in which we live and set out to find the gifts of that world, rather than to force the world to change to fit our old patterns. In a witnessing community, leadership is always needed because the job it seeks to do is always bigger than the resources. Therefore, it must search out the ways that training and education can continue creatively, not by crying over the fact that there are not enough people with the right training to do the work, but by working and participating with those who are willing to serve Christ and their brothers.

3. A catechism of participation

In a modern world where men cannot even pretend to know the answers, a catechism based on answers is obsolete. In Chapter 4 we saw that a catechism was not always questions and answers, but began as a living dialogue between the instructor and the catechumen who was "instructed in the way of the Lord" (*katēchēmenos,* Acts 18:25). However, by the sixteenth century it was developed into a doctrinal handbook. Following earlier beginnings, Luther wrote a catechism for children in 1529 which set a pattern for childhood education which still exists in the Roman Catholic Church and in some Protestant churches.[9] This pattern of questions and answers needs to be radically revised if it is to be relevant in the twentieth century.

In his book *The Church Inside Out,* Hans Hoekendijk has suggested that a modern catechism would have to "lead us on a course of thinking things through with question after question after question, thus inviting us to search things out for ourselves."[10] Carrying this idea one step farther, we can say that the way we will learn to think with openness to the future and courage to live with questions and next questions is by a catechism of participation. *A catechism of participation will raise the questions of life in the context of a witnessing and serving community so that men will be able to learn to think by participating in the thinking of the community as it in turn participates in the dialogue between God and the world.* A participating catechism would have three parts: community, fun, and the Bible.

Such a catechism would at least be on the way to answering two problems that Paul Tillich raises in relation to religious education.[11] He says that one problem is that we give answers to questions not raised instead of letting the student raise his own questions. A catechism of participation would make possible what Tillich calls *human-*

istic education which aims at the development of all human potentialities as the student is nurtured in a community which itself is constantly asking questions about the world in which it lives and about how they are to join in God's mission in that world. The student would be able to ask his own questions as he joined with others in searching for, not answers, but the next set of questions in his life. The other problem that Tillich raises is that of properly interpreting the symbolic character of religious language without losing the power of the symbol. Again a catechism of participation would at least be moving in the right direction as it not only helped the student to learn *technical* skills of Biblical and historical understanding but also *inducted* him into the world as understood as the arena of God's activity. In such a context, symbols would have reality, because they would express the actuality of life of the student and teacher as they served Christ in the world.

Theologically speaking, a participating catechism of community, fun, and the Bible should start with the Bible and God in his self-revelation; but educationally speaking, it starts where man is in his world and helps him to see what God is doing as he participates in a community that has "eyes of faith." At any rate, this participation catechism is a "spiral curriculum" that goes round and round through all the life of the Christian as he participates in Christ's invitation to join in God's mission.

The first part of the participating catechism is *community* in a threefold sense. It is the community as the world where the student lives each day. It is the community as the peer group and production group who form the patterns of his daily life. It is the community as the witnessing community that participates with him in the world where he lives and in the social groupings of which he is a part. The community that forms the context of his learning to understand his world as God's world is the witnessing community. Here he comes to understand the meaning of service, the meaning of solidarity, the meaning of the fact that God cares for him as a father cares for his children. When this community is unable to express by its life the catechism of witness and service, then the student never learns the right questions. He is still asking: Where is God? Why should I love others? Who am I? Who is my neighbor? at age eighty because he never participated in a community that lived out the answers to those questions. Only in such a community of concern can the student move on to the next questions of: How can I love God? What can I do for my neighbor? How can I teach others that they are important because God loves them? How can I work for justice and reconciliation? These questions in turn only move on to the next questions, where the student can participate in all sorts of risky attempts to live out the answers through concrete actions in and through the social structures of society.

The second part of the catechism of participation is *fun*, in every sense of the word. The gospel is a celebration of freedom (see Part V). God has set his people free. Men are able to live sustained by Christ's love in a world where the power of evil has been defeated, if not yet vanquished. A student must be able to participate in this freedom and joy if he is to be able to know that in fact "for freedom Christ has set us free" (Gal. 5:1). If the community in which he participates is bound by meaningless rules and customs, he will have the same experience as the Gentile Christians who found that their Jewish brethren expected them to become Jews in order to become Christians (Acts, ch. 15). And their questions will be in terms of questioning outward restrictions rather than questioning how to bring freedom to all men.

Not only is the gospel a word of joy, but also education needs to be a word of enjoyment. Long ago, Augustine suggested in his writings about Christian catechism that *hilaritas* was the sphere of catechetics and the rule for the catechist was, "God loves a cheerful giver" (II Cor. 9:7).[12] Luther tells us: "If we wish to train children, we must become children with them. Would to God such child's play were widely practiced (which teaches knowledge of scripture and God)."[13] And in our time, when there is much concern about motivation of learning, it is being suggested that people learn best when the excitement and the interest in the learning process itself motivate them.[14] Nor does it take educational experts to tell us what we all have experienced—that the things we have enjoyed most in our lives are the things that we remember with warmth and tenderness and that provoke an instant response of interest whenever they are mentioned. Just look at the face of a sailing enthusiast when you begin to speak of frostbite racing at Larchmont, or at the face of an old Eagle Scout when you talk about taking the boys on an overnight.

An adequate catechism of participation will involve the student in so many moments of joy celebration, parties, events, and fun as part of the witnessing community that he will believe that the relationship of love between God and his children is worth asking questions about. His response, when you begin to talk about "church life," will not even be recognizable when compared to the normal look of boredom that appears when the subject is mentioned to most people who have been nurtured in churches whose outworn structures and customs have killed off both participation and joy, and seem to be threatening to "kill off God."[15]

The third part of the catechism of participation is the *Bible*. The Bible is the record of God's self-revelation, and it is through the Biblical record that we hear Christ's invitation to join in God's action of reconciliation, and we are nurtured in the Christian life (I Tim. 3:14–16).[16] A catechism of participation includes the student's participation in the Bible in several different ways. He must be given countless opportunities to learn of the mighty acts of God in his relationship with man and history and the world by joining in programs of drama, study, song, and art that teach the story through participation. He must be helped to grow so familiar with the story of the Bible that in fact he becomes part of the story: he participates in it; it is his story because the people are his people, his family. He must be given opportunities to participate in the Biblical story made real as it is lived out in the day-to-day experiences of the witnessing community. Without constant participation in the dialogue of the Bible with the world in which he lives, the student will be unable to receive the "eyes of faith" to be able to discern God's action in searching for his answers and next questions.

Such a catechism of participation may sound vague, but it is a lot more real than one written on paper with questions and answers. An example of the way this catechism has functioned in one particular family-type witnessing community and one particular series of incidents may help to see its meaning more clearly.

In the East Harlem Protestant Parish, one of the churches, in following the *Daily Bible Readings,* studied Exodus and the story of freedom for thirteen weeks.[17] It was studied in house Bible study groups; preached about on Sunday; studied by the youth, complete with freedom songs, a mock march to Washington, and an exodus extravaganza; studied by the children with tambourines for Miriam, burning bushes that really burned, golden calves of Clorox bottles, and freedom trees with the symbols of the exodus hung on the branches.[18] The people in the entire community were doing it, talking about it, and applying it to the problems of freedom in their own world. They were having a "ball" singing about it, acting it out, making "in" jokes, etc. The people in the whole community were definitely learning the story as they went back over the events of deliverance each week to remember what God and Moses had been doing and to see what they would do next.

Finally, at the end of the study, it was decided to invite all the different parish units to celebrate the sixteenth anniversary of the parish with a service of worship and a family potluck dinner for two hundred people. The theme of the dinner became "Sixteen Years in the Wilderness." Decorations, music, etc., were arranged accordingly. The youth collected all the skits they had done into one long drama of freedom, complete with Moses in a baby carriage, a cardboard sea that opened and closed, and Miriam's dancers. Everyone enjoyed the play immensely, even when the bush, which was made of cardboard, nearly burned up. The youth had a chance to make a real contribution to their church family, and most people knew the words of the play even when they could not hear them for the laughter. Even the children were involved, for they had made most of the scenery and knew the songs and the story. The next day two four-year-olds who had attended the festivities were overheard talking together. One child dressed in a green bathrobe said to the one in a red bathrobe, "Will you let my people go?" The red-robed boy replied, "Yes," to which the child in green said with great disgust, "You're not supposed to say that!"

Nor did the community, fun, and Bible catechism end with the festival. Soon afterward the adults and youth were called to work for freedom in their own community by organizing a school boycott and conducting a freedom school. Some of the best freedom fighters were the younger youth who spent hours putting out flyers, canvassing, etc. All the children participated in making picket signs in church school and joining in a freedom parade. From this work in the boycott emerged an independent civil rights group committed to work for quality integrated schools. It took as its symbol the freedom trees that the children had made in their study of Exodus, now decorated with an "equal" sign instead of bush, sea, manna, and tablets. The young people and adults became interested in learning more about Negro and Puerto Rican culture and in the summer conducted a freedom school for youth, with such community programs as one sponsoring the star of *West Side Story,* Chita Rivera, and a complete homegrown musical production of the play. From this developed a continuing program of "Nites on the Town" to attend plays, concerts, art exhibits featuring Negro and Puerto Rican artists. And a year later a teen-ager who was being interviewed on television concerning his interests told of how he helped teach the children and used crafts as a means of helping them remember the lesson. When he was asked what sort of crafts they made, he could not remember even one! But thinking back to the kinds of things we did in the peer-group program, he said, "Like if you studied George Washington Carver, you would make a 'peanut tree.' " Thus the catechism of community, fun, and the Bible goes on and on, because it is a catechism of participation—participation in a witnessing community in the world.

9

PARTICIPATION IN A STYLE OF LIFE

1. Participation in a style of life

PARTICIPATION IS THE METHOD by which Christ shapes our lives. Through sacramental actions he unites us to himself and to one another so that we grow up into Christ. "Rather, speaking the truth in love, we are to grow up in every way into him who is the head, into Christ, from whom the whole body, joined and knit together by every joint with which it is supplied, when each part is working properly, makes bodily growth and upbuilds itself in love" (Eph. 4:15–16).

As we grow up into Christ, he is shaping our daily actions and habits into a Christian style of life. In a world of change we need to ask ourselves, What does this style of life look like as we participate in a Christian community in a secular world? Our physical habits of eating, dress, talk, work, social life, give each of us a certain style. Our commitment to Christ helps him to shape this style into habits and ways of life that are helpful to us in being able to serve him in the world. As we seek to make our patterns of Christian living functional in terms of our continuing relationship to Christ and involvement in the world, we face two dangers. One is that we will fail to recognize that style is always changing to fit the particular situation in which we live. Then we make habits into laws, and style into privilege instead of servanthood. The other is that we will fail to recognize that, although patterns of obedience change with the world, obedience to Christ does not change. It is this constant relationship to Christ that enables him continually to shape our lives.[1]

In Acts 2:42-47 we have what is considered the classic statement of the style of the Christian life. But, taken in itself, this description is misleading because it is a static description of the life of the church that Luke includes as part of his overall theme of a "church on the move" witnessing to its Lord. The reason for this static description at this point in the story (Acts, chs. 1 to 5) seems to be that Luke is describing the dawn of the New Age and wants to give a summary of life together that exhibits the presence of Christ in the midst of the church, before he tells what happens as they follow him in his way into the world. They are already on the way. They have followed him from Galilee and Jerusalem and have found him risen and "on the move" in Emmaus, Bethany, and the Mount of Olives (Luke 24:13, 50; Acts 1:12). And Luke pauses briefly in the story to describe their life together before he shows how that life is lived together as they follow their Lord "to the end of the earth" (Acts 1:8).

A second thing that is misleading about Acts 2:42-47 as a pattern is that it is not intended as a static pattern or standard. There can be no set pattern because in Luke's view the church is the place where people are called to encounter Christ and respond, and this response can take many shapes.[2] Luke intends his description of the elements of church life to show the response and witness of the people to the presence of their Lord and the power of his Spirit. It is the Lord who creates the church and adds to its number (Acts 2:47). He also intends to show that by the power of Christ's Spirit the Christian community fulfills all the ideals of Greek and Israelite community life. For this reason he gives another description of their life together in Acts 4:32-37.

Luke summarizes the response in terms of four aspects of life together. One is that as they gather in Christ's presence he continues to teach them through the *teaching of the apostles* (Acts 2:42–43). This same witness continues today as communities of Christ learn of the victory of God's love in the Bible and continually witness to this love in the world. Another response to the presence of Christ is that their *fellowship or participation* (sharing of common life) with each other is exhibited in sharing of possessions with all who have need (Acts 2:42, 44–45). The overflowing of love that results from Christ's gift of his Spirit is that all of life is at the disposal of others as a gift to their need. A third response is that of the *breaking of bread* as a continuation of the meal with their risen Lord (Acts 2:42–46; Luke, ch. 24). In this meal they continued to participate with Christ in the power of his death and resurrection. The fourth response of the people was that they continued in *prayer and praise* of God as a spontaneous expression of their joy in the presence of the Lord (Acts 2:42, 47).

This is Luke's picture of the style of life of the early church. What should be the style of communities of Christians who live after two thousand years of following the Lord toward his final completion of the New Age? I suspect that our patterns will have many similar characteristics for we are involved in following the *same* Lord who is at work participating in the *same* mission of God to complete his plan of redemption of the world. Yet perhaps more can be gained as a starting point to thinking about our own style if we look at the two underlying intentions of Luke's description. His first intention was to describe the style of life of a church "on the move," of a pilgrim people who were participating in the mission of the Lord in the world. The second intention was to describe the joyous response of men and women to the presence of their living Lord as a fulfillment of the longing of all men for true community life. Neither of these intentions sets the exact pattern of living. Rather, they describe the context of a witnessing community in which men and women participate as Christ trains them for God's mission. And it is from this participation in a living dialogue between the presence of God in Jesus Christ in their midst and the mission of God in the world that the style of life of any particular witnessing community emerges.

2. The purpose of a style of life

The purpose of a style of life is mission—God's mission. Its purpose, regardless of its pattern, is to allow Christ to shape and mold our lives so that we may be equipped to join in God's mission of making men truly human.[3] From this it follows that it should help to make us more truly human (more able to love and obey and serve God and to love and serve our fellow human beings). Thus rather than setting us apart from other men, it should assist us in living with them, participating in the life of the world as a leaven that seeks to point to God's desire for the true humanity of every man.[4]

Because the purpose of style is mission, it should always be functional, and the particular disciplines or habits of life that go to make it up should be functional. A witnessing community may have a particular discipline or habit structure of life, but this must always be related to the function of the group as it serves in the world. There are three possible approaches that a witnessing community may take toward *discipline*. One is to ignore it altogether and see what emerges as the shape of the lives of its members as they participate in the dialogue between God and his world. This is a very attractive approach in our time, because we are so afraid of any type of piety or planned style that will separate us from life in the world. Thus a task force group in city government may decide to concentrate on listening and learning and let the questions of discipline and style remain questions as they get on with the work. This is an honest approach because, indeed, we have only a few hints about what it might mean to live as a secular Christian in a secular world. However, the danger of this procedure is that the nurture of a witnessing community depends on the willingness to keep our lives open to Christ as well as to the world, and ignoring the question may result in a kind of style that tends to close off opportunities to hear and see God's mission. No matter how much a community refuses to adopt a conscious style of life, the question cannot be completely ignored, because a style emerges out of their daily habits of living and serving together, and they have to consider whether this style, be it one of complete individualism, assists them in their task of mission.

A second possible approach to discipline is to make certain requirements for membership in the witnessing community that consciously seek to set the style of the group. This, for instance, is the approach of the group ministry in East Harlem, and of the Church of the Saviour in Washington, D.C.[5] But this approach is only valid if the discipline is seen as an essential form of equipment for a particular mission. The East Harlem Group Ministry has a discipline because they know that there is no possibility of being responsible human beings in the tasks that they have to perform without regular periods of Bible study, retreats, worship, and involvement together in issues of social action, economics, and vocational commitment. The disciplines are *ad hoc* to this task, the task that all the members, both lay and clergy, of the group share in common, that of working as staff in one of the Christian communities serving the area of East Harlem.[6]

A third possible approach to discipline in a witnessing community seeks to take discipline seriously while recognizing that the main way that it shapes people's lives is through their participation in a witnessing community.

Thus the witnessing community will take real thought as to the pattern of its life together that will help it to be most open to Christ and God's mission in the world, but it will not make this pattern a requirement for participation in the community. Rather, it will seek to help shape each person's life as he participates, letting each person grow in his habits of Christian obedience in the same way that a child grows in a family. In this way, participants are loved into loving, helped into helping, served into serving until they are "hooked" on a particular pattern of life. The danger of this approach is that it has to be able to take a positive group approach to learning by participation, without taking the negative approach at the same time, which assumes that those who do not learn by doing and adopt a certain pattern are wrong or to be rejected.

Variety in approach to discipline is a given in a situation where discipline is functional and grows out of involvement in God's mission. Thus a family-type community will be most likely to adopt the third suggestion just because of its emphasis on nurture of people from all age groups and walks of life, while a structure of permanent availability or a task force structure might be more likely to adopt a wait and see attitude or a strict discipline related to its task. At any rate, discipline is not a set of rules. It is a set of habits of Christian living that enable men to participate more fully in God's mission. And because it is made up of human habits, it is continually in the process of change, taking shape around the interaction of the actions of men and women in the world and what they consider to be the source of their action in God.

3. *Participating in style as it opens our lives to God*

If the suggestions made concerning Luke's intention in writing Acts 2:42–47 are correct, they lead us toward a new angle of vision on style of life. Here we see that the particular activities or habits of the early church were understood as part of their response to the presence of their Lord as they sought to follow him into the world. As they participated in the dialogue between God in Christ and his mission in the world, their lives were shaped by the presence of Christ and their eyes were opened to see and understand what he was doing in the world. So, *style of life means style of mission,* in which the witnessing community participates, on the one hand, in habits that open its life to God and, on the other hand, in habits that open its life continually to the world. Because God is in continual dialogue with man and the world, these two focuses are never separate, but have a dialogical relation to each other as we allow our understanding of style to take shape from the way God is at work in the world.

Although all habits of the Christian life are in a continual process of change just because they are *human* habits and are part of the whole process of life and history, the relationship to God in Christ that these habits express does not change. God has revealed himself as Father of all his children through the history of Israel and of Christ and his church. This self-revelation forms the basis of any participation in style as it opens our lives to God. Thus the witnessing community finds that it comes to know God as he has chosen to be known—through the Scriptures and the Sacraments. This is not to say that God is not known in an infinite variety of ways by the power of his Spirit, but merely to say that the witnessing community must take seriously the source of its eyes of faith and the source of its nurture as found in the gifts of Scripture and Sacraments. For it is here that we come to know what God's mission is and receive the power and strength to join in that mission.

The *Scriptures* contain the story of God's action in history to create a community in which men might be restored to their true humanity in a relationship of harmony and trust with God and other men. In the story of God's action we are enabled to see the way he is at work reconciling man to himself and each other through Jesus Christ. Living continually with the Bible in study, discussion, listening, and prayer will help us gain eyes of faith so that we may see Christ's action of reconciliation in the world around us and know where to follow him.[7] God is in dialogue with his world and one of the parts of this dialogue is the record of salvation history. When we stop listening to that record through serious study, thought, and discussion of the Bible, we cut ourselves off from openness to what God is saying. When we are listening, his word will come to us in many and unexpected ways that guide and enlighten our actions. Perhaps the moment when the book of The Acts speaks to us is when we are preparing a lesson plan by discussion with others who share the same jail cell as a result of a civil rights protest. Perhaps Psalms will become a living word only when we hear them sung accompanied by trumpet, drum, and dance. Perhaps Isaiah's words will best come alive when we study them in the summertime with a group of people out in the park rather than on Christmas Eve by candlelight. Who knows how the words will speak? All we know is that God's promise is that he does speak, and that his words do not return to him empty (Isa. 55:11).

The *Sacraments* are signs given by Christ by which God declares his love for us and makes us his people. In the Sacraments of Baptism and Communion, the people know and participate in the work of God's love through the death and resurrection of Jesus Christ, so that they may have eyes of faith to know and participate in God's action in the world. As God's people, we receive *new life* because in the washing with the water God frees us from the power of sin, and in the breaking of bread our forgiveness is continually renewed until our new life is completed when Christ comes again. As God's people, we receive a *new Lord* because in Baptism he claims us as his own and gives us a new Christian name, and in Communion we are united with him in the eating and drinking by the power of the Holy Spirit. As God's people, we receive a *new community* because in Baptism the witnessing community adopts us into the family, and in Communion the community is joined together around the Lord's Table. The Sacraments form a center to the worship and action of a witnessing community because they unite God's action both past and present with our own response both present and future. His acts of salvation bring to us the gift of forgiveness and healing and hope that we carry out in the world.

The particular form of the Sacraments needs to change in various situations, times, places, and communities. But they remain the heart of the Christian life because here Christ invites us to participate with him in his life and work. Without the Sacraments, Christian education has no heart, for here is the center of participation in Christ's invitation to join in God's mission; here is the new life essential for joining in God's work of making all things new. In spite of all the discussions concerning the origins of Baptism and concerning its flagrant misuse in the traditions of the church, it still remains an important part of the life of the witnessing community. For there must be a means by which men and women and children respond to the gospel, a means by which they say, "Yes, I want to accept Christ's invitation to join in God's mission."[8] How Baptism is administered and to what age should depend on the type of witnessing community.

I suspect that infant Baptism should only be administered in a family-type structure. Here infant Baptism would be a living illustration of what the family of nurture is all about. God welcomes all who wish to be a part of the community whether they are able to be of help or not. By his grace, all people are welcome, including children, invalids, alcoholics, prostitutes, addicts, neurotic mothers, domineering fathers, and overrich businessmen. By his grace all are accepted and nurtured in Christ. Secondly, children should be a part of a family community and any child whose parent is a member of the community should also be considered a full member if the parent so desires. In addition, children who have reached the age of wanting to join things and be part of them by eight to ten should also be welcomed as full members of the family community even if their parents have no interest in being members themselves. Thus they, like everyone else, can be part of the nurturing and sustaining fellowship of the Christian family with opportunities for growth and service, and further opportunities to declare their commitment to the service of Christ and the world as they grow older.

In the other types of witnessing community where membership depends on the task to be performed, it is assumed that those being baptized would at least be old enough to join in the community's task or function. It would be a denial of the *ad hoc* character of these groups if babies and young children were baptized in these congregations. None of the communities is trying to be the whole church, everything to everyone. Therefore, people can easily belong to more than one community if they so desire, as, for instance, a businessman who belongs to a task force community where he works and also belongs to a family-type community with his wife and children. In any case, a witnessing community should only baptize those people whom it feels capable of nurturing within the function of its mission. The new life that is born in Baptism needs an appropriate community in which to grow.

Communion should be the center of life of every witnessing community if it is at all possible, for it is the Sacrament by which Christ equips us for his work. If this is not possible, a Christian will need to belong to at least one community where he can participate frequently in the Lord's Supper. The Communion meal is Christ's offering to his people and should be open to all who wish to receive this gift of love. Christ did not think that anyone was so separated from God's love that he should not be invited to the feast (Matt. 7:9–11; 22:1–10). The abundance of God's mercy is that it is freely offered to all, as the Father offers good gifts to all his children. Certainly Communion is a serious affair as Paul reminds us (I Cor. 11:17–32). But he also reminds us that it is the Lord who judges, and we only can judge about our own selves and why we are at the Table. The reason to come to the Table is not because we are worthy, but because we are unworthy. "Not because we are righteous, but because we sincerely love our Lord Jesus Christ and desire to be his disciples."[9]

4. Participating in style as it opens our lives to the world

At the same time that the witnessing community participates in habits that open its life to God, it also participates in those habits which open its life to the world as it takes part in the dialogue of God with the world. Because the world is always changing and in process, the habits that open the lives of the community to service in that world are always changing. All we can do is suggest habits or qualities of life that at present seem helpful to the lives of some communities as they seek a style of life in a secular world. As the world changes, these will change. For instance, the habit of service following our "servant" Lord is fairly obvious, yet its meaning is bound to have radical shifts as the modern technological age enters the age of cybernetics. What will service mean when everyone has enough to eat, clothes to wear, a guaranteed annual wage, and nothing to do? Perhaps then service will mean allowing other people to have the enjoyment of serving you! Perhaps it will mean finding ways of meaningful use of leisure time. In our time God is no longer *deus ex machina* to solve insoluble problems. In the future he may no longer be a *deus ex machina* to provide us with people to serve in the sense of their being physically in need. Then service will mean something different. For the habits that keep our lives open to the world have to be always changing along with the world itself.

Service is especially important in the world today that is weary of hearing about love and fellowship and wants to see healing and service at points of real need and brokenness in our society. For this reason our actions of service to our brothers are not only a spontaneous outpouring of the love and mercy that God has shown to us, but also signs of the presence of God's healing power in the brokenness of the world (Matt. 11:1–6). Yet the Christian community can make no claim to be the only servant in society. It shares with all men both concern and talent for making the world more human. All acts of healing, reconciliation, love are signs of God's concern for his world, not just those performed by the Christian community; and frequently the skill, commitment, and quality of the actions of service are far better among non-Christians (Matt. 25:31–40). The habit of service for the Christian cannot stem from desire for reward because there is no way to earn God's love which is freely given. It cannot stem from desire to do a better job than others because it has no "corner on the market "of talent for service. The habit of service stems simply from the following of a Lord who came to be the servant of all and wanting to join in his work of service in the world (Phil. 2:6–8; John 13:15–16; Matt. 20:26–28).

The habit of service needs to be learned by participating with others in a serving community. There is no time when people are too young or too old to learn, and the more opportunity they have for joining in the serving of others, the more they will learn to serve as a natural part of their lives. Study and discussion of the meaning of service and of stewardship (the way we use our money and time to serve others) is also important.

One peer group had a lesson devoted to stewardship and service with which they made a folder with slots for six new pennies that were named according to their use in the church and in the world. As the children completed the folders they were given pennies for the slots. After the discussion, an offering was taken in which each child was asked to decide what part of that six cents he should keep and what part he should give to help a family with no food and rent money. Many, especially girls, put in all the pennies. Others were reluctant to part with any. One little girl, who knew her mother actually had no money for food or rent, put in one penny. Her friend teased her unmercifully for her stinginess all the way home, but she kept the pennies tight in her hand. When she arrived home she was nearly in tears, but she went to her mother and said, "I brought you five cents to help buy some milk!"

Another habit of life that keeps us open to the world and to God's presence in the world is the habit of *seeking*. Seeking is the quality of freedom, joy, and hope that is part of the Christian life. Because we are sure of God's love for us and for his world, we are free to share that love without fear that anything can happen that will separate us from God's love (Rom. 8:38–39; ch. 9). Because we live in the time after the resurrection when our risen and victorious Lord is with us in the world, we can live in the world affirming with joy and thanksgiving by our words and actions that Christ is Lord of the world. Because we have confidence that God has a plan and purpose for our lives and for the world, we can live with hope in his continuing presence in history and the events of our lives. Seeking is looking at the world with eyes of faith. As we come to know God's action in Scripture and Sacrament and join in that action as part of a serving community, we grow to have eyes that constantly seek out what God is doing so that we may be present with him. Everyday wonderful things are happening all around us, and if we walk with our eyes and hearts open, we will find many occasions to pray to God "on location," rejoicing in the partial signs of God's rulership (Eph. 5:15–20).[10] They appear both in small ways, such as an act of kindness, or a moment of accomplishment, or joy shared with a brother, and in large ways, such as international treaties and new cures for disease and social ills. Everyday events of difficulty, judgment, failure, and hatred are signs to us of the need for Christian action and prayer as we join in God's mission. Yet with eyes of faith we seek out these signs as well that we might find ways of being instruments of peace and reconciliation among people, groups, and in the great social and political divisions of our time.

Seeking makes us flexible and open to the world of change in which we live, for having already received the sign of God's love in Jesus Christ, we are willing to adapt our style of life to the world in which we live so that our actions as a Christian community may be relevant signs of God's love (Luke 11:29–36; I Cor. 9:19–23). Seeking is the context of prayer, for it is here in the world, day by day, that we speak to God confident of his presence and concern. We pray to him as we see signs of need and of our own weakness. We pray to him at the signs of joy. Our lives are lived in constant expectation that what happened on the Emmaus road is bound to happen over and over to us. We run to look out of the window, we walk down the street expectantly, we approach a difficult meeting or task with openness to new possibilities because we are seeking out the mission of God wherever, whenever it may occur in the world in which we live.

As we participate with Christ in the world, our lives are shaped by the habit or quality of *solidarity*. This quality of solidarity grows out of our understanding ourselves as men created in complete interdependence and our experiencing the possibility of interdependence as we participate in a witnessing community. God created us to live in community with others and with God. He has re-created us by the love of Christ so that we might be forgiven our own self-love and helped to live once more in community (participation) and harmony with others (I Cor. 10:16–17). The world cries out for a way to find this harmony among men asking, "How can I live with my brother?"[11] The Christian community is called to be a sign to the world that this is possible in spite of all weaknesses by the power of God (Matt. 5:13).

The quality or style of solidarity in our lives grows as we follow him who gave his life for others (John 15:12–17; Matt. 20:25–28). Jesus' solidarity was with all men, for he not only received sinners, he was baptized on their behalf (Luke 15:2; Matt. 3:15). We too have solidarity with all men, for we live together in God's world in mutual interdependence and in mutual need of forgiveness.[12] Out of this knowledge, then, we cannot help standing in a relationship of forgiveness and mutual concern with our brother. We also have solidarity with all men because we stand in need of strength. In the Christian community we find that no man has to bear his burdens alone (Gal. 6:1–5). Solidarity means that no matter how weak we are and how great our burdens, in Christ we find the strength to help carry someone else's burdens, and to go much more than halfway in seeking to break down barriers of separation between ourselves and other people (Matt. 5:38–42).

As we continually participate in Christ's love, our love for our brothers also grows, and we learn to share our life together with them in the witnessing community. We learn to share our work together doing what needs to be done without concern for prestige or authority. Writing a play or making a speech becomes a matter of common concern even if there is only one author or speechmaker. Sweeping the floor and cleaning up are not left to the person whose job it is if we can do it together. We learn to share happiness and fellowship together as we accept one another as we are. Parties become fun because with or without drinks we enjoy being together and just acting natural. We learn to be honest with one another, able both to correct and to encourage one another in love and solidarity (Eph. 4:5).

One example of growth in the habit of solidarity can be seen in a day spent together at a retreat center to prepare a task force on remedial reading for their job in the coming fall. As the various people worked and talked together about their job, they discovered a sense of teamwork and solidarity in spite of the fact that the group included teen-agers from prep schools and slums, Catholic nuns, atheists, Jews, college intellectuals, public school teachers, and housewives. In discussing together, writing lesson plans together, washing dishes together, they found a beginning of the solidarity needed to do their job as they participated in God's mission of making men truly human.

Secularity is a style of Christian living that is important in any age because it represents a refusal to be dominated by man-made religious customs (Matt. 12:1-8; I Sam. 21:1-6), a refusal to use religious practices as a means of trying to make God do our bidding (Matt. 23:1-2; Gen. 11:1-9), and a refusal to live as slaves to custom and superstition when we have been freed to be sons of God by the gift of Christ's love (Gal. 4:1-7). But the style of secularity is doubly important today because we live in a secular age, an age in which society and culture are no longer dominated by a religious or metaphysical point of view.[13] Secularity means that we participate in a world where we feel free to work out our own destinies and his-tories, both because we are men of a world of science and technology and because we are men who have confidence in God's action in and through the history of this world. God has created us to have dominion over the world and made us partners in shaping its history (Gen. 1:28).[14] We are his sons who by the power of Christ are secular men who no longer need to live in fear of change and fate (Gal. 4:3). Instead, as God's sons, we are free to join him in the task of making the world a place where men may find true human community and freedom.

Like Paul, who insisted that men did not have to become part of the Jewish culture and be circumcized in order to be Christians, we must insist that modern man does not have to adopt a religious or metaphysical world view in order to be Christian (Acts, ch. 15). Where the world is come of age, the style of a witnessing community should be that of a world come of age—secularity. This style is shaped as the community is a community truly added unto (*paroikia*) the secular world. The witnessing community knows that its "commonwealth is in heaven," that it belongs to God and his mission, and therefore it can be added onto any culture and any situation where God calls it to serve (Phil. 3:20). If the world that it serves is secular, then the men also who labor with Christ in that world should be secular, insisting that men live honestly in their own time and history and seeking to fight against any new ideologies that try to force men to live and think in a closed world.[15] Secular Christians are free men—free to smoke, drink, dance; and free not to smoke, drink, dance; free to wear a gray flannel suit, or free to wear a beard; free to read *The Saturday Evening Post, Esquire, Playboy;* free to be snobbish intellectuals; free to be antichurch civil rights workers—in short, they are free to be themselves as part of the world in which they live subject only to consideration for their neighbor and for the job that Christ has called them to do (I Cor. 10:23–24).

Shalom can be part of the style of the Christian life simply because it represents what the world would like to be and what God intended it to be in this New Age (Rom. 8:19–20; Matt. 11:1–6). The Hebrew word *shālōm,* is usually translated "peace" in English, but it has a much fuller meaning in Hebrew thought. It is generally used to describe the benefits of peace, wholeness, fertility, and prosperity that God grants his people. Such blessings are described over and over in God's promises to the patriarchs (Gen. 12:1–3).[16] For Israel the condition for peace was the presence of God (Isa. 45:7–8). Christians were quick to see Christ as the "Prince of Peace" because he came to fulfill God's promise of peace and harmony to the world (Isa. 9:1–7; Luke 2:14 to 19:38). And in the New Testament, "God's shalom is the most elementary expression of what life in the new aeon actually is" (Matt. 11:1–6).[17]

Shalom, like all the qualities of the Christian life, is a gift of Christ. It represents what all life should be and can be by the power of Jesus Christ—complete wholeness and peace in relationship to God, the world, other men, and ourselves. Shalom is an accomplished fact in God's promise and fulfillment of that promise in the death and resurrection of Jesus Christ (Jer. 29:11; John 14:27; Eph. 2:11–22). It is a present reality when Christ is present in our lives with concrete gifts of healing and wholeness (Acts 10:36; Heb. 13:20–21). It is a future hope because, although it is realized only partially now, we live in the confidence of the Messiah's completion of his work in the world when "he will speak peace to his people" and "glory may dwell in our land" (Ps. 85:8–9). Because shalom is a relationship of harmony between ourselves and God and the world, it includes all the qualities of the Christian life and could be said to be the basis of any particular style of life. Scripture helps us to know God's action in bringing shalom to the world. Sacraments and service enable us to participate in this action both at the Lord's Table and in the world. Seeking gives us eyes of faith to discern moments and events of shalom wherever they break into our world. Solidarity helps us to live out shalom in relationship to our brother. Secularity recognizes that shalom is to be found in God's world and not in an artificial religious setting. Whatever the particular habits of a Christian community by which it opens its life to God and the world, they will all contribute to the gift of shalom, a gift of Christ to those who participate in his life in the world.

Because style grows out of participation in Christ, it is always a gift of Christ. It is he who nurtures and shapes our lives and grants to us the power of life to grow as his disciples. It is strange to think of style as a gift because it is just the sum total of all the little habits and actions and thoughts of life that make up who we are in our relation to God and the world. Yet we can speak admiringly of a woman who has "real style" because of the sum total of her particular habits and way of carrying herself. We know that a person really has to work at doing things in a particular way to develop style, but we also know that the total result of "real style" is a gift that only some people possess. Thus Christian style involves real work on concrete habits of obedience, yet as a totality it is made up of qualities that finally are gifts from God. It is also strange to think of style as a gift because it is an expression of the words of Jesus, "take up your cross and follow me" (Matt. 16:24). The way of the cross is not always easy, and style is the way the cross of Christ shapes our lives by allowing us to participate in his life of suffering and serving love. It is the way the cross stretches out our lives into the suffering and ambiguities of the world and our fellowmen in service and solidarity with them, and the way the cross stretches our lives "up or down" toward God as the source of all our life and growth.

PART FIVE

The Purpose of Christian Education—
Celebration

Matthew 25:31–40

"When the Son of man comes in his glory, and all the angels with him, then he will sit on his glorious throne. Before him will be gathered all the nations, and he will separate them one from another as a shepherd separates the sheep from the goats, and he will place the sheep at his right hand, but the goats at the left. Then the King will say to those at his right hand, 'Come, O blessed of my Father, inherit the kingdom prepared for you from the foundation of the world; for I was hungry and you gave me food, I was thirsty and you gave me drink, I was a stranger and you welcomed me, I was naked and you clothed me, I was sick and you visited me, I was in prison and you came to me.' Then the righteous will answer him, 'Lord, when did we see thee hungry and feed thee, or thirsty and give thee drink? And when did we see thee a stranger and welcome thee, or naked and clothe thee? And when did we see thee sick or in prison and visit thee?' And the King will answer them, 'Truly, I say to you, as you did it to one of the least of these my brethren, you did it to me.' "

The parable of the Last Judgment is found in the final section of Matthew (chs. 19 to 25) and some people doubt whether this parable was actually told by Jesus. Yet it contains ideas that are so amazingly original that it is difficult to imagine who else would have told it.[1] Jesus' expression of love for the poor is very characteristic (Mark 9:37, 41). Although other writings contain descriptions of Judgment on the basis of good deeds, there is no other parallel to Jesus' idea that there is no way to earn our way into heaven because we do not even know when we are doing good deeds. Jesus addressed this parable to his disciples to urge them to recognize that God's rule means obedience. The secret of discipleship is learning to extend to others the abundance of mercy and forgiveness that we have experienced (Matt. 18:23–35). Judgment has already been revealed as Christ's disciples are asked daily to respond in such spontaneous love to Christ and to their neighbor. Yet justification and participation in God's Kingdom is offered to the non-Christian on the basis of his fulfillment of the same law of love and forgiveness (Rom. 2:14–16).

The total effect of this parable seems to be one of doom for disciples (and for members of organized Christian churches) who can never be such "spontaneous servants"; and joy for those who, without knowing the name of the Lord, simply serve their brother. Yet, in fact, it is a parable of freedom for the Christian, for here the Christian is set free to serve. He is set free for spontaneous service by the simple fact that, because he can never know when he is doing good deeds, and because there are always others who are clearly doing a better job of service, there can never be a way of earning his way into God's Kingdom. There is nothing left to do but simply to serve and love even as Jesus loved and served, and to celebrate the fact that men are helped, the lame walk, the blind see as signs of the New Age of Christ in our midst (Matt. 11:1–6). The purpose of Christian education is that Christians may be set free to celebrate in this manner—that they may be so filled with the love of Christ, so sustained by him in his mission of reconciliation in the world that they are free from themselves to be men for others.

CELEBRATION OF FREEDOM

1. *The purpose of Christian education as celebration of freedom*

THE PURPOSE OF Christian education is celebration of God's mighty acts of salvation by which he has saved his people and set them free. To participate in Christ's invitation to all men, women, and children to join in God's mission of restoring men to their true created humanity by reconciling them to himself and one another is simply to participate in an invitation to freedom and the celebration of that freedom.[1] We saw in Chapter 3 that Christian education and mission are both words that refer to the nature and function of the church as it participates in God's sending and saving work.[2] Both mission and Christian education take their shape from God's activity, which is basically one of leading men from bondage to freedom. As Hans Hoekendijk points out in his article, "Mission— A Celebration of Freedom," mission "is a continual and universal Jubilee, a persistent celebration of freedom, opening up future and hope. In one sentence: it is playing off the feast of liberation against all the facts of bondage."[3] If mission is a jubilee, a celebration of freedom, so too is Christian education, for it is participation in the same liberating mission of God. And so its purpose is that men might live with joy in celebrating what God has done and is doing in their lives.

The structure of this celebration, like the structure of

education, is that of dialogue. It is a dialogue between God and his world as actions and promises of salvation are realized in the events of history.[4] The witnessing community joins in the dialogue by listening to the way God has revealed himself in the past and seeking out and pointing to God's saving work in the present. This participation of the witnessing community in the dialogue of celebration between God and his world is expressed in its *worship life,* for in its life of worship, the community celebrates the events of salvation so that God's name may be glorified and Christ's name may be demonstrated in their midst (Ps. 100; Matt. 18:20). At the same time, the participation of the witnessing community in the dialogue of celebration between God and his world is expressed in its *life of service,* for in its life of service, the community celebrates the events of salvation so that God's name may be glorified and Christ's name may be demonstrated in their midst (Matt. 5:16; Rom. 12:1–8). Celebration, then, finds its structure in a dialogue between witness and service as the movement back and forth reflects the community's participation in God's mission. Thus Christians worship and serve God along the way in the world and find the points of their celebration as the "happenings of God" are known along the way. The names of the locations may be different from the Red Sea, Sinai, Shechem, Emmaus, Corinth, but they will still be locations of celebration on the way to the end of the earth. The time of the celebration may not be the time of Unleavened Bread, Passover, or Pentecost, but the time will still be part of God's history on its way to fulfillment. And the witnessing community will continue to live day by day in celebration, following their Lord with joy and leaving the long-range plans and directions up to him (Acts 2:37–42).

2. *Celebration of freedom for God*

The worship life of the witnessing community is the way in which it expresses its freedom for God. God is the source of the community's life and salvation. He is the source of their freedom from fear, selfishness, limitations, and failures. Therefore, they gather to celebrate his saving action as it has been known in the past and it is known in their lives. This worship has no set form or pattern, but rather, it takes its form from the dialogue of celebration between God and his world that it seeks to express. The worship of the Christian community is celebration of Communion because in the one loaf, the unity of men in Christ is celebrated, and in the "breaking of bread," Christ's own Messianic banquet is spread for all the world to share. The worship of the Christian community is celebration of culture because here the world in all its wonderful and varied forms is offered to God as a "living sacrifice." The worship of the Christian community is celebration of confession because here men see most clearly the sharp edges of life where their own sin and inadequacies are known, and confess the name of one whose love was so great that "he gave his only Son" (John 3:16).

When we speak of worship as *celebration of Communion,* we are looking at the Sacrament of the Lord's Supper from the point of view of mission.[5] If we are looking at it theologically, we would have to explain all the many meanings and origins of the Communion. If we are looking at it ontologically, we would have to explain its being and existence. But looked at from the point of mission, Communion is simply the celebration of God's missionary purpose of reconciling the world to himself. In Communion the community celebrates the death and resurrection of Christ and participates in the promise of that victory by the power of Christ's spirit.[6] It celebrates the fact that "all mankind is marked by God's power over sin and death, . . . with freedom, joy and hilarity."[7] The power of God's reconciliation in Jesus Christ has already made all men our brothers, so that Communion itself is a celebration of the new humanity that belongs to the whole world with the conviction that the gift of unity has already been given in hope that what is realized now as promise will finally be fulfilled. The act of Communion is the sign to all the world of the purpose of God's love in uniting all men in Jesus Christ.

There is no one way to conduct the service of Communion as long as it is a Communion service of celebration, as long as the people know that they are in fact participating in Christ's Messianic banquet which God has spread for the whole world to share. The meal should be as simple as possible, using the one cup and the one loaf as a symbol of the fact that we are so glad to be one, and to love one another, that germs and such have no relevance.[8] The actions of the meal should reflect what is actually happening by letting the people gather together around the table to eat and letting them serve one another. The Communion should be shared so frequently and the liturgy itself should be so simple and informal, that people will forget to worry about whether Mr. Jones drops the bread or Mrs. Cruz wears a hat. Not only the Communion but the entire service should have an atmosphere of informality and mutual involvement that would be found at a family banquet.

One way to encourage an understanding of worship as a celebration of Communion is to express the celebration of the Communion or participation together in other parts of the service as well. In the East Harlem Protestant Parish two important ways of doing this are the "Concerns of the Church" and the "Handshake of Fellowship." The Concerns of the Church are a time when the whole congregation has a chance to talk and to make announcements about the activities of the week, to ask for prayers, and to tell about items of mutual interest, such as a housing rally, a school meeting, or a birthday. God's concern for the whole world is made clear here by concrete examples of the life the congregation shares with the world which it serves. By the time the congregation finishes sharing its life together, not only the prayers and sermon but also the Communion becomes an offering up to God of the concern of the congregation for its participation with Christ in God's mission of reconciliation. The Handshake of Fellowship takes place before the Communion as an expression of the "kiss of peace." During the singing of a hymn, everyone goes around and shakes everyone else's hand to make them welcome at the Table of the Lord. When new members join the church, this is the time when the whole congregation comes up and welcomes them and extends the right hand of fellowship to take part in Christ's ministry in the world. Through such actions the people come to the Communion Table to celebrate Communion with Christ having already participated in celebration of their life together.

Another way to encourage an understanding of worship as celebration of Communion is to act out the parts of the service in such a way that they can be seen and felt by the people. A parade down the street waving palm branches is worth a hundred psalms of praise. The following year the dried palms, which are returned to the church on Ash Wednesday to be burned as a symbol of how promises turn to dust and ashes, are worth a hundred prayers of confession. A service of "foot washing" in which the minister kneels down and polishes the shoes of the congregation is worth a hundred sermons on how the job of *minister* and congregation is to be a servant. A congregational meal that acts out the events of the Last Supper, including eating and drinking together at tables, is worth a hundred articles about how Communion remembers not only Christ's death and resurrection but also the night in the upper room. An informal play of the story on the road to Emmaus put on by the elders of the church in place of the sermon, in which they talk together about not having read the *Jerusalem Times* and not being up on the latest news and about how the "women always see crazy things and carry false tales," is worth what Communion is worth—especially when "Jesus" invites the whole congregation to be part of the drama and to break bread with him in the upper room.

But the most important way to encourage worship as

celebration of Communion is to have Communion whenever the community is able to gather for its worship as a means of celebrating their mission.[9] In one witnessing community the people earned the name for themselves of "Sunday–Wednesday Christians" from those who were scornful of the weekly pattern of Sunday worship and Wednesday Bible study that was so important to its members. Gradually over the years, however, they learned that the way to be "Sunday through Saturday Christians" was to begin the week at the Lord's Table seeking strength and help for the service in the world the whole week long. When Communion is viewed this way—as a means of joining in God's mission, as a means of receiving the strength and power to be his witnesses, as a means of involvement with Christ in the work of his world—then it becomes celebration—a celebration of God's mission.

The worship of the Christian community is a *celebration of culture* because it includes all the gifts of the congregation that they bring as an offering to God. If worship takes place "along the road," as the community follows its Lord in witness and service, then it takes place in and through the events of the road and the culture of those who are celebrating those events. This is the meaning of the incarnation, that Christ is present with his people in concrete human ways and not only in one way or cultural form.[10] The worship of God is shaped by the witnessing community, its life, its culture, the world around it, and its function in that world as it serves Christ. It is a celebration of all of life.[11] The two focuses of worship as a celebration of culture are the need for concrete relevance and the need to demonstrate the "breaking down of barriers" in Jesus Christ.

Relevance means relevance to the congregation and to its function in the world. A congregation could worship in its own language, sing the songs that it enjoyed, and have services according to its own life rhythm. But this would make the worship relevant only to itself and not necessarily relevant to the world or to its function in the world (I Cor. 14:8–19). The witnessing congregation needs to express in its worship the witness that it is called to make the world in terms which the world can hear. If a task force group is involved in a ministry to blind children, its worship should be through group participation in actions and words. If a community is a family-type community, its worship should include many elements that allow children and other uninformed people to participate with no need for extensive preparation. If a congregation is situated in a cosmopolitan urban setting, it should express the variety of religious traditions that are found in the cultures of the people, even if it means singing Bach, a Spanish carol, a gospel hymn, and rock 'n' rock all in the same service.

The "breaking down of barriers" in celebration of culture means that no particular culture and no particular "cultic" act can be considered to be the only standard for worship. Even if the congregation is unlucky enough to include people who are generally from the same cultural background, it should constantly strive to enrich the background and break down old stereotypes by including gifts of worship from other cultural groupings. Because in Christ we are all one, it is all right to sing a Negro spiritual if we are not Negro, or to have an Ash Wednesday service if we are not Catholic. Because we are one in Christ, it is important to celebrate our unity by having worship led by all different members of the congregation. They are a living symbol of the fact that in worship, as in the congregation, there is both minister and layman, young and old, male and female, white and Negro, strong and weak. What is important is that the services celebrate the richness of culture that is open to us by providing opportunities for celebration of both unity in Christ and freedom in Christ as a relevant witness to the world.

The worship of the witnessing community is a *celebration of confession* because it is an opportunity for men to gather and make public confession of their sin and of their faith. Anyone who has ever been part of a community that sought to help its members take up their cross and follow Christ knows how difficult this is. Life is full of rough edges. There is no point in the participation in God's mission when his people are unaware of their inadequacy for the tasks or their need for strength and forgiveness. Even in moments of almost complete joy, the rough edges seem to have a way of appearing either through some sudden personal flare-up, or some little tragedy or incident, or in our own minds as we remember that shalom is only in bits and pieces in our lives and that this moment of joy will turn into other moments not so enjoyable. In fact, strangely enough, it is the mixture of joy and sorrow that makes many moments of celebration wonderful.[12] So it is in celebration worship. In the very moment of joy in remembering the love of God and praising his name, we also remember who *we* are and how much we stand in need of "heaven's mercy and help." We come as the blind, and lame, and poor to the Table of the Lord, trusting in his righteousness and not in our own, celebrating the fact that God by his acts of salvation accepts us although we are unacceptable.[13]

True confession is a celebration, for it happens only in a relationship of confidence and love. A child confessing to his mother that he broke her best coffee cup is delivered from his misery by the act of the confession itself as his mother gives him a chance to make amends, to try again, to wash the dishes the next night. So it is with us. The moment of confession when Christ's word is heard and received is a moment of celebration and opportunity for new life. In the same way it is a moment of gratitude and confession of the name of him who lives and forgives so that all the world might know the greatness of his love.

The worship of the witnessing community in all its aspects is a celebration, a celebration of God's action in loving and redeeming his world through Jesus Christ.

3. Celebration of freedom for the world

The participation of the witnessing community in the dialogue of celebration between God and his world is expressed in its life of service. This service, along with witness, is the purpose of Christian education, for we participate in Christ's invitation to witness and service in order to celebrate what God has done and is doing for us and the whole world. Service is a celebration of Christ's yoke of freedom, "For my yoke is easy, and my burden is light" (Matt. 11:30). He shapes our lives and fits our lives to his yoke so that we may be able to share in his Messianic task of bringing freedom and wholeness to all men. Service is a celebration for the same reason that the yoke is easy, because it is a service of love shared with Christ and our brothers on behalf of all men. Those whose lives are shaped to the yoke in the witnessing community know that service can be celebration, for they have experienced the joy of knowing that when they help others, their actions are not only used by Christ as signs of his Kingdom, but also their actions actually do serve the Lord whom they love, who is present in their neighbor in need (Matt. 25:31–40). To catch a glimpse of the joy of serving when it is done in love and for love, just think of the last time you did something very difficult for someone you loved purely out of the joy of pleasing him. The act itself was a celebration of your love.

There are certain barriers to the joyous service of others. One is the barrier of a church community that expects its members to spend all their free time serving the church and attending church functions, and thus makes it impossible for the members to be available "for others." Another is the fear and lack of self-confidence people have. They are sure others do not need help or will reject them in their offer of service This fear is real, because many times we do get rebuffed in individual offers of help, many times we are unable to do a job, and many times we involve ourselves in a course of action in a social issue where others take differing sides. A third barrier is simply selfishness or the feeling that it is better to take care of one's own self-interest.

A final barrier is that of misunderstanding cultural patterns. Often men and women are unable to serve because the witnessing community asks them to serve in ways that are foreign to their way of life or training. For instance, in a culture of poverty, being paid to render a service to others is not a sign of lack of generosity, but rather, a sign of solidarity, respect, and dignity, and of the community's confidence that the person can do the job. A small payment to a teacher or canvasser or office assistant will mean that the worker feels important enough and wanted on the team enough to come and do his job on time and learn to take on more and more responsibility. Paying the person in that situation is a way of freeing him to serve with newfound confidence and ability.

Such barriers and others like them are not easily overcome, but at least they are put in the right perspective when service is viewed as the work of the whole witnessing community. Then, at least, those who are afraid, selfish, ignorant find others to help them and stand with them in the effort to place their lives at the disposal of others. Then, at least, the whole community can try to understand the particular barriers that it faces and try to structure its life toward involvement in the world in the light of the talents of its members and the needs of the community that it serves.

It is difficult to participate in the celebration of freedom *for* the world unless you begin by learning the freedom from self that enables you to serve others. Sometimes starting is the most difficult part. The human mind is far more agile at making up excuses and binding us with imaginary chains of immobility than it is at making us get up, get out, get in, and serve. Yet growth in Christian maturity means growth in freedom from self and for others, and a beginning must be made over and over again. Here the community is the essential context of this growth in maturity, for it is the love of the community that breaks through the chains of inactivity.

Once the habit of service begins to grow, the joy of service will grow with it until it becomes a normal part of life. When this begins to happen, this is a sign that Christ is at work in the midst of the community to nurture *spontaneous Christians*—Christians who serve willingly with the joy and love that Christ has given to them in their hearts. The nurturing of spontaneous Christians should be the purpose of any Christian community, for its desire is so to participate in extending Christ's invitation to join in God's mission that this invitation will be heard and accepted with joy. When this joy is real, the Christian's style of life will be one of spontaneous witness. Like the disciples on the road to Emmaus, Christians will run the seven miles to Jerusalem with joy just to tell others the good news. Like the sheep in the story of Matt., ch. 25, they will help others and not even know they are helping, because it is so much a part of their life. Such spontaneous Christians are born, not made, born of Christ's spirit which alone can give new life and growth to maturity. The context of this spontaneity is the witnessing community, and such birth becomes a possibility only when that community itself is engaged in joyous celebration of God's love by its service to the world.

4. Celebration Education

Christian education as the participation with Christ in inviting men to join in God's mission of making men truly human takes place in the context of a witnessing community. Its structure is shaped by the dialogue between God and his world. Its method of education is that of participation in the witnessing community in the world. But its purpose is celebration—the celebration of what God has done and is doing in the world by means of witness and service. Such education is *celebration education*. It cannot be otherwise, for it is no education at all unless it is a participation in the joy of the Lord. And those who try to make it less than celebration are guilty of denying God's good gifts to his children and offering them a *stone* instead of the *bread of life* broken in celebration of the victory of Christ (Matt. 7:9–11).

NOTES

Introduction

1. Letty M. Russell, Clyde Allison, and Daniel C. Little, *The City—God's Gift to the Church* (Division of Evangelism, The United Presbyterian Church in the U.S.A., 1960).

2. Paul S. Minear, *Eyes of Faith* (The Westminster Press, 1946).

3. James Barr, "Revelation Through History in the Old Testament and in Modern Theology," *New Theology, No. 1,* ed. by Martin E. Marty and Dean G. Peerman (The Macmillan Company, 1964), pp. 60–74. Barr makes a case for re-evaluating the idea of salvation history, but largely succeeds in establishing that it is important to be aware of other motifs, and that salvation history may not always be a relevant tool of apologetics.

4. Thomas Wieser (ed.), *Planning for Mission* (The United States Conference for the World Council of Churches, 1966). A collection of working papers prepared in connection with the Missionary Structure Study. See also the reports of the Western European and the North American Working Committees, published in 1967 under the titles *Church for Others* and *Church for the World;* and J. G. Davies, *Worship and Mission* (SCM Press, Ltd., 1966).

Part I. Christian Education—A Gift of God's Love (Matthew 7:9–11)

1. Joachim Jeremias, *The Parables of Jesus* (Charles Scribner's Sons, 1956), p. 119.

148 CHRISTIAN EDUCATION IN MISSION

Chapter 1. Christian Education as Bread Instead Of Stone

1. Robert Lynn, *Protestant Strategies in Education*, Monographs in Christian Education, ed. by C. Ellis Nelson (Association Press, 1964), Chs. 1 and 2.

2. *Ibid.*, p. 23.

3. George Albert Coe, *A Social Theory of Religious Education* (Charles Scribner's Sons, 1917), p. 6.

4. Lynn, *op. cit.*, p. 54.

5. Frederick Maier, "A New Direction for the Educational Enterprise" (working papers prepared for the Board of Christian Education of The United Presbyterian Church in the U.S.A., April 8, 1965).

6. John Fry, *A Hard Look at Adult Christian Education* (The Westminster Press, 1961), p. 96.

7. *Youth in the Ghetto* (Harlem Youth Opportunities Unlimited, 1964), pp. 236–244.

8. I. A. Muirhead, *Education in the New Testament*, Monographs in Christian Education, p. 63. Thomas F. Torrance, *The School of Faith* (Harper & Brothers, 1959), p. xxxii.

9. Fry, *op. cit.*, p. 69.

10. *Ibid.*, p. 138.

11. Charles H. Dodd, *The Apostolic Preaching and Its Developments* (Harper & Brothers, 1936).

12. Muirhead, *op. cit.*, pp. 23, 48.

Chapter 2. Christian Education in the Context of a World of Change.

1. C. von Krockow, *Soziologie des Friedens* (Stuttgart, 1962), pp. 125 f.

2. Arend T. van Leeuwen, *Christianity in World History*, tr. by Hubert H. Hoskins (London: Edinburgh House Press, 1964), p. 403.

3. Gerhard von Rad, *The Theology of Israel's Prophetic Tradition*, Vol. II of *Old Testament Theology*, tr. by D. M. G. Stalker (Harper & Row, Publishers, Inc., 1965), p. 106.

4. Van Leeuwen, *op. cit.*, pp. 331 f. Van Leeuwen quotes Friedrich Gogarten, who defines secularization as "human existence [that] comes to be determined by the dimension of

time and history." A recent book on Gogarten is Larry Shiner, *The Secularization of History* (Abingdon Press, 1966).

5. Von Rad, *op. cit.,* pp. 101, 361. Von Rad points out that this characteristic Old Testament view of history as open to the future continues as a philosophy of the modern world that views mankind as moving toward fulfillment.

6. Harvey Cox, *The Secular City* (The Macmillan Company, 1965), p. 264.

7. Fry, *op. cit.* This fact is assumed all through the book which draws on secular educational literature to support the arguments concerning the need for educational reform in the church.

8. See Ch. 1, Sec. 1.

9. H. H. Groothoff, *Pädagogik, Fischer Lexikon* (Hamburg, 1964), Vol. 36, pp. 77 f.; Coe, *op. cit.,* p. 16; Edgar Z. Friedenberg, *Coming of Age in America* (Random House, Inc., 1965), p. 221.

10. Lynn, *op. cit.,* p. 80.

11. Hans Hoekendijk, "Morphological Fundamentalism," in Wieser (ed.), *op. cit.,* p. 134.

12. *Youth in the Ghetto,* p. 357. See also *The Education of Minority Group Children in New York City* (Harlem Parents' Committee, 1965), p. 34; Jerome S. Bruner, *The Process of Education* (Vintage Books, Inc., 1960), p. 70.

13. Ronald Gross and Judith Murphy, *The Revolution in the Schools* (Harcourt, Brace and World, Inc., 1964), p. 2.

14. *Ibid.,* p. 4.

15. Solon T. Kimball and James E. McClellan, Jr., *Education and the New America* (Random House, Inc., 1962), pp. 17, 164.

16. Bruner, *The Process of Education,* p. 17.

17. *Ibid.*

18. *Ibid.,* pp. 12–14. For further development of Bruner's ideas on education, see Jerome S. Bruner, *Toward a Theory of Instruction* (Harvard University Press, 1966).

19. Kimball and McClellan, *op. cit.,* pp. 266–268.

20. J. C. Hoekendijk, *The Church Inside Out,* tr. by Isaac C. Rottenberg (The Westminster Press, 1966), pp. 79 f.

Part II. The Context of Christian Education—A Witnessing Community (Deuteronomy 6:4–9, 20–25)

1. G. Ernest Wright, "Deuteronomy," *The Interpreter's Bible,* 12 vols., ed. by George A. Buttrick, *et al.* (Abingdon Press, 1951–1957), Vol. II, p. 372.
2. *Ibid.,* p. 378.
3. Von Rad, *op. cit.,* p. 394.

Chapter 3. No Education Without a Witnessing Community

1. Karl Barth, *Church Dogmatics,* 4 vols., ed. by G. W. Bromiley and T. F. Torrance (Edinburgh: T & T Clark, 1956–1958), Vol. IV, Part 2, § 67, pt. 1, p. 617. "The Christian community, the true Church, arises and is only as the Holy Spirit works—the quickening power of the living Lord Jesus Christ. And it continues and is only as He sanctifies men and their human work, building up them and their work into the true Church."
2. Philip B. Gove (ed.), *Webster's Third New International Dictionary of the English Language* (G. & C. Merriam Company, Publishers, 1961).
3. Lewis J. Sherrill, *The Gift of Power* (The Macmillan Company, 1955), p. 45.
4. Yves Congar, *The Wide World, My Parish,* tr. by D. Attwater (Helicon Press, Inc., 1961). Congar's book deals with the important problem of the salvation situation of those outside the Roman Catholic Church, and the tension between the church in the world and yet over against the world. See also *De Ecclesia; The Constitution on the Church of Vatican Council II,* ed. by Edward H. Peters (Paulist Press, 1965), Ch. II, "The People of God."
5. Suzanne de Dietrich, *The Witnessing Community* (The Westminster Press, 1958), p. 16. See also M. Richard Shaull, "The Form of the Church in the Modern Diaspora," *New Theology, No. 2,* ed. by Martin E. Marty and Dean G. Peerman (The Macmillan Company, 1965), p. 285. Shaull suggests that our time calls for "smaller communities of witnesses, dedicated to this task of witnessing to the reality of God's grace in the world and calling men to receive it and live by it."

6. Neil G. McCluskey (ed.), *Catholic Education in America* (Columbia University Press, 1964), p. 109; Coe, *op. cit.*, p. 87; "The Religious Educators: Their Vision of Polity and Education," *Union Seminary Quarterly Review* Vol. XXI, (Jan., 1966).

7. Paul Lehmann, *Ethics in a Christian Context* (Harper & Row, Publishers, Inc., 1963), p. 85.

8. "Christ the Hope of the World," Report of the Advisory Committee of the Evanston Assembly of the World Council of Churches, quoted by Colin Williams, *Where in the World* (National Council of Churches, 1963), p. 43.

9. Hans J. Margull, *Hope in Action*, tr. by Eugene Peters (Fortress Press, 1962), p. 180.

10. Hoekendijk, *op. cit.*, pp. 22 f.

11. *Institutes of the Christian Religion by John Calvin*, tr. by John Allen (2 vols., Presbyterian Board of Christian Education, 7th American Edition), IV.i.5.

12. Martin E. Marty, *Babylon by Choice* (Friendship Press, 1965), p. 56.

13. Letty M. Russell, "Changing Structures in the East Harlem Protestant Parish," *Union Seminary Quarterly Review*, Vol. XXI (March, 1966).

14. Wieser (ed.), *op. cit.*, pp. 208–214.

15. Alan Richardson, *History, Sacred and Profane* (The Westminster Press, 1964), p. 259. "The Christian understanding of the disclosure of God's purpose in history [is] a disclosure which in every generation remains to be discovered through the opening of the eyes of faith."

Chapter 4. Education in a "Family of God" as a Witnessing Community

1. Otto J. Baab, "Family," *The Interpreter's Dictionary of the Bible*, ed. by George A. Buttrick, *et al.*, 4 vols. (Abingdon Press, 1962), Vol. II, pp. 238 ff. See also "Household of God," p. 658.

2. Barth, *op. cit.*, Vol. IV, Part 2, p. 637. "But in its New Testament form Christian ethics is never concerned only with the requirement of an abstract private morality but always with instructions for the edifying of the community."

3. Thomas Ralph Morton, *Household of Faith* (Glasgow: The Iona Community Publishing House, 1951), p. 31; Johannes Pedersen, *Israel: Its Life and Culture*, 2 vols. (London: Oxford University Press, 1926 and 1940), Vol. I, p. 51.

4. Morton, *op. cit.*

5. George MacLeod, *We Shall Rebuild* (The Westminster Press, 1945), p. 39.

6. "Martin Luther's Preface to the German Mass," *Works of Martin Luther* (Muhlenberg Press, 1932), Vol. VI, p. 173.

7. Letty M. Russell, "The Family and Christian Education in Modern Urban Society," *Union Seminary Quarterly Review*, Vol. XV (Nov., 1960).

8. Talcott Parsons, *Essays in Sociological Theory*, revised ed. (The Free Press of Glencoe, Inc., 1949), pp. 180 f.

9. Warren Asby, "Caste and Class in the Local Church," *Theology Today*, Jan., 1957.

10. Kimball and McClellan, *op. cit.*, p. 148; Peter Berger, "The Second Children's Crusade," *The Christian Century*, Dec., 1959.

11. Alex Blöchlinger, *The Modern Parish Community*, tr. by Geoffrey Stevens; adp. by Hilda Graef (London: Geoffrey Chapmann, Ltd., 1965), pp. 132 ff.

12. See Ch. 5, Sec. 1.

13. See Part IV.

14. Lewis Joseph Sherrill, *The Rise of Christian Education* (The Macmillan Company, 1950), pp. 186 ff.; Augustine, *The First Catechetical Instruction*, tr. by Joseph P. Christopher (Ancient Christian Writers, No. 2), (The Newman Press, 1946).

15. Blöchlinger, *op. cit.*, p. 133. Quoting Yves Congar he states that the parish is a family structure where the priest has a "fatherly" rather than governing role to play. The bishop, representing Christ, is the head of the parish and plays the governing role.

16. Hans Hoekendijk, Lecture, Union Theological Seminary, New York, Nov. 18, 1965.

17. Blöchlinger, *op. cit.*

18. Barth, *op. cit.*, Vol. IV, Part 2, § 67, pt. 1, pp. 636 f.

19. See Ch. 8, Sec. 2.

20. Peter Berger, "The Christian in the Structures of Mod-

ern Society." Unpublished speech at the North American Conference on Missionary Structures, World Council of Churches, New Haven, Conn., 1963.

Chapter 5. Education in Other Forms of Witnessing Communities

1. Hans Hoekendijk, Lecture, Union Theological Seminary, Nov. 11, 1965; Marty, *op. cit.,* p. 56.

2. Hans Hoekendijk, "Comments on the Missionary Structure Study," *Concept* (Papers from the Department on Studies in Evangelism, World Council of Churches), VII, p. 5.

3. Sidney Mead, "Denominationalism: The Shape of Protestantism in America," *The Lively Experiment* (Harper & Row, Publishers, Inc., 1963), Ch. VII, pp. 103 ff.

4. George Casalis, "The Church—A Segment of the World," in Wieser (ed.), *op. cit.,* pp. 122 f.

5. Siegfried von Kortzfleisch, *Mitten im Herzen der Massen* (Stuttgart: Kreuz-Verlag, 1963), pp. 191 ff.

6. Arthur G. Smith, *Group Ministry* (Westminster, Church Information Service, 1965), p. 15.

7. Elizabeth O'Connor, *Call to Commitment* (Harper & Row, Publishers, Inc., 1963), p. 34.

8. Lyn Tornabene, "The Way-Out Minister of Washington Square," *Dominion,* Nov., 1965, pp. 16–19.

9. *Ibid.,* p. 17. "Seventy-five percent of the congregation [of a hundred members] work for non-profit organizations."

10. Hartmut Dreier, "Reflections of the Present Ministry of the Parish," East Harlem Protestant Parish Board Report, May, 1964.

11. Tornabene, *loc. cit.,* p. 18.

12. Charles B. Mercer, "Thoughts on Relocation" (a discussion of Metropolitan Associates of Philadelphia, MAP), *Concept,* IX, p. 1.

13. Kimball and McClellan, *op. cit.,* pp. 266–268.

14. See Ch. 9, Sec. 1.

15. Letty M. Russell, *Christian Education Handbook* (East Harlem Protestant Parish, 1966); C. Ellis Nelson, Lecture, Union Theological Seminary, 1961, Ch. 4, p. 9.

16. For further information concerning description of such

attempts at new types of structures, see *Planning for Mission* and the Report of the North American Working Committee, World Council of Churches entitled *Church for the World*.

Part III. The Structure of Christian Education—Dialogue
(Luke 24:13–35)

1. Hans Conzelmann, *The Theology of St. Luke,* tr. by Geoffrey Buswell (Harper & Brothers, 1960), pp. 9–17.

2. Von Rad, *op. cit.,* p. 107.

3. Conzelmann, *op. cit.,* p. 203; William Robinson, *The Way of the Lord,* a doctoral dissertation submitted to the Theological Faculty of the University of Basle (Basle: William Robinson, Jr., 1962), pp. 61–69.

Chapter 6. Dialogue with Eyes of Faith

1. Maier, *loc. cit.,* p. 7.

2. Paul Lehmann, Lecture at Union Theological Seminary, Feb. 22, 1966.

3. Reuel L. Howe, "The Dialogical Foundations for Christian Education," *An Introduction to Christian Education,* ed. by Marvin J. Taylor (Abingdon Press, 1966), p. 88.

4. *Webster's Third New International Dictionary.*

5. *Ibid.*

6. Bruner, *The Process of Education,* p. 7; see also Ch. 2, Sec. 2, of this book.

7. Donald E. Miller, "Psychological Foundations for Christian Education," in Taylor (ed.), *op. cit.,* p. 54, calls this a perceptual theory of learning which emphasizes knowing the underlying perceptual pattern that guides the content.

8. Bruner, *The Process of Education,* p. 13.

9. Reuel L. Howe, *The Miracle of Dialogue* (The Seabury Press, Inc., 1965), pp. 35, 66. Howe defines dialogue as "that address and response between them in spite of all obstacles which normally would block the relationship." He says that the purpose of dialogue is "the calling forth of persons in order that they may be reunited with one another, know the truth, and love God, man, and themselves."

10. Webber, *op. cit.,* pp. 74 ff.; Torrance, *op. cit.,* pp.

xliii ff. Torrance indicates that Reformation theology is dialogical because it involves the address of the Word of God and the obedient response of faith. "Dialogical theology arises within the Church as the sphere of the two-fold conversation between God and His people, and between members of the Church in the presence of the Word and Truth Himself." (P. xlvii.)

11. Harrison S. Elliott, *Can Religious Education Be Christian?* (The Macmillan Company, 1940), Ch. 3.

12. Letty M. Russell, *Daily Bible Readings* (East Harlem Protestant Parish quarterly).

13. Howe, "Dialogical Foundations," in Taylor (ed.), *op. cit.*, p. 91.

14. See Ch. 9, Sec. 3.

Chapter 7. Dialogue in Natural Social Groupings

1. Thomas Wieser and J. Gordan Davies, "Introductions," in Wieser (ed.), *op. cit.*, p. 5.

2. Kimball and McClellan, *op. cit.*, pp. 266 ff.

3. Morton, *op. cit.*, p. 74.

4. Gerald H. Slusser, *The Local Church in Transition* (The Westminster Press, 1964), p. 79. Slusser indicates that success is no longer a powerful symbol. It has been replaced by social acceptance from one's fellowmen.

5. Abbé Michonneau, *Revolution in a City Parish* (The Newman Press, 1950).

6. See Ch. 8, Sec. 1.

7. James D. Raths and Jean D. Grambs (eds.), *Society and Education* (Prentice-Hall Inc., 1965), p. 72.

8. See Ch. 9, Sec. 1.

9. *Youth in the Ghetto,* p. 373. "Be it delinquent or nondelinquent, an attractive sub-culture fashioned with thoroughness and imagination enables the participant to begin to think about a career line of advancement."

10. Russell, *Christian Education Handbook.*

11. *Youth in the Ghetto,* p. 371. "In these [youth] programs the impetus to achievement . . . will be the demands and pressures of one's peers rather than one's remedial teacher or social worker."

12. See Ch. 8, Sec. 2.

13. Letty M. Russell, "Equipping the Little Saints: An Emerging Pattern of Christian Education," *Adult Teacher*, Jan.–Feb., 1961 (Board of Education of The Methodist Church).

14. Howe, *op. cit.*, p. 76.

Part IV. The Method of Christian Education—Participation
(I Corinthians 10:16–17; 11:23–26)

1. John A. T. Robinson, *On Being the Church in the World* (The Westminster Press, 1962), p. 132; S. V. McCasland, "Body," *The Interpreter's Dictionary of the Bible*, Vol. I, pp. 451–452.

2. William F. Arndt and F. Wilbur Gingrich (eds.), *A Greek-English Lexicon of the New Testament* (The University of Chicago Press, 1957).

Chapter 8. Teacher and Student Participation

1. Robert Lynn, "The Religious Educators: Their Vision of Polity and Education," *Union Seminary Quarterly Review* Vol. XXI (Jan., 1966), p. 149.

2. *Ibid.*, pp. 150 f.; Coe, *op. cit.*, p. 64.

3. Sherrill, *The Rise of Christian Education*, pp. 86 f.; John Calvin, "Geneva Catechism, 1541," Question 308; Torrance, *op. cit.*, pp. 53 f. Calvin explains that Christians need continual instruction by the pastor because "we must continue to be disciples of Christ right to the end. But He has ordained the minister of the church to teach in his name."

4. Maier, *loc. cit.*, p. 7.

5. Howe, *op. cit.*, p. 76; Miller, in Taylor (ed.), *op. cit.*, p. 56.

6. See Ch. 7.

7. Letty M. Russell, "Christian Education in the Inner City," in Taylor (ed.), *op. cit.*, pp. 267 ff.

8. Russell, *Christian Education Handbook*, pp. 44 ff.

9. Gerard S. Sloyan (ed.), *Shaping the Christian Message* (The Macmillan Company, 1959), p. 3.

10. Hoekendijk, *op. cit.*, p. 80; Hans Hoekendijk, "Sign

of the Cross—Mark of Cain," *Union Seminary Quarterly Review*, Vol. XXI (May, 1966).

11. Paul Tillich, *Theology of Culture*, ed. by Robert C. Kimball (Oxford University Press, 1959), Ch. XI, "A Theology of Education," pp. 146 ff.

12. Augustine, *The First Catechetical Instruction, loc. cit.* p. 17.

13. Luther, "Preface to the German Mass," *loc. cit.*, p. 176.

14. Bruner, *The Process of Education*, p. 73; Bruner, *Toward a Theory of Instruction*, p. 73. "If there is self-reward in the process [of learning] it is in the sphere of 'doing things for merriment,' particularly things that might otherwise be too serious."

15. Fry, *op. cit.*, p. 5. Fry is so pessimistic about the state of education in the churches that he warns against trying to make it easy by promising adults that it will be fun! Yet according to Bruner, fun is an intrinsic motivation for learning. (Bruner, *Toward a Theory of Instruction*, p. 114.)

16. See Ch. 6.

17. Russell, *Daily Bible Readings*.

18. Russell, *Christian Education Handbook*, pp. 52 ff.

Chapter 9. Participation in a Style of Life

1. James Blackie, "The Pattern of Christian Living," *Student World*, Vol. LVI (1963), pp. 65 ff.; Russell, *Daily Bible Readings* (Lent, 1966).

2. Thomas Wieser, "The Church and the Way of the Kingdom," in Wieser (ed.), *op. cit.*, pp. 16 ff.

3. Maier, *loc. cit.*, p. 6.

4. Leslie W. Brown, *Relevant Liturgy* (Oxford University Press, Inc., 1965), p. 8. Brown quotes Masao Takenaka in saying, "The starting point of the indigenization of Christian faith is not so much in the field of architecture or music or art, not even in theology, but in the field of Christian style of living in contemporary Asia."

5. O'Connor, *op. cit.*, p. 34.

6. "Disciplines of the East Harlem Group Ministry" (East Harlem Protestant Parish, Revised, 1962).

7. See Ch. 6, Sec. 3.

8. See Ch. 3, Sec. 3.

9. See Ch. 10, Sec. 2.

10. Robert Raines, Lecture, Union Theological Seminary, Feb., 1966.

11. Horst Symanowski, *The Christian Witness in an Industrial Society,* tr. by George H. Kehm (The Westminster Press, 1964), p. 50. "Luther's question when he was in, and even after he had left, the monastery [was]: 'How can I find a gracious God?' . . . But another question does drive us around, unsettles us, agitates whole peoples, and forces us into anxiety and despair: 'How can I find a gracious neighbor?' "

12. John J. Harmon, "Life Together in the City," *The Catholic World,* Aug., 1965, p. 322. "God has so fashioned his creation that existence is always, at every point, already mutual and interdependent."

13. *Study Encounter,* "Secularization and Conversion," Vol. 1 (1965).

14. Cox, *op. cit.,* pp. 263 ff.

15. *Ibid.,* pp. 153 f.

16. Pedersen, *op. cit.,* Vol. II, p. 313.

17. Hoekendijk, *op. cit.,* p. 21.

Part V. The Purpose of Christian Education—Celebration (Matthew 25:31-40)

1. Jeremias, *op. cit.,* p. 144.

Chapter 10. Celebration of Freedom

1. Thomas C. Oden, *The Community of Celebration* (Board of Education of The Methodist Church, 1964), p. 12. "Authentic human existence may be understood as an act of celebration."

2. See Ch. 3, Sec. 2.

3. Hans Hoekendijk "Mission—A Celebration of Freedom," *Union Seminary Quarterly Review,* Vol. XXI (Jan., 1966), p. 14.

4. Barth, *op. cit.,* Vol. III, Part 4, p. 378. "To be joyful is to expect that life will reveal itself as God's gift of grace,

that it will present and offer itself in provisional fulfillments of its meaning and intention as movement."

5. In this chapter *Communion* and *service* are discussed from a perspective different from that of Chapter 9. There they are discussed as "style"; here, however, they are discussed in the perspective of "celebration."

6. H. Grady Hardin, Joseph D. Quillian, Jr., and James F. White, *The Celebration of the Gospel* (Abingdon Press, 1964), p. 13.

7. Harmon, *loc. cit.*, p. 327.

8. The celebration of Communion is beyond the question of germs for the same reason that any love relationship is beyond that question. We seldom refuse to kiss those we love because they sneeze once or twice, although we may refuse to kiss them, for their sake, if we have a cold. Thus in Communion we drink together without concern for the others' germs, although we may not drink on occasion when we are sick, out of consideration for the others.

9. David M. Paton (ed.), *The Parish Communion Today* (London: S.P.C.K., 1962), p. 111. "The celebration of the liturgy must mean a dedication to the mission. The true worshipper goes out of liturgy into mission, inevitably, for this is how he is to understand going out of the church into the bent and bungled world."

10. John A. T. Robinson, *Liturgy Coming to Life* (The Westminster Press, 1960), p. 35.

11. Harmon, *loc. cit.*, p. 326.

12. Oden, *op. cit.*, p. 122.

13. Harvey Cox, "Beyond Bonhoeffer," *Commonweal*, Sept. 17, 1965. "The church will make mistakes and it can and must repent. As the church of Peter [Bonhoeffer insists] it not only confesses Christ; sometimes it betrays him and always it is . . . forgiven."